The Jesus of History as the Christ of Faith

Daniel Liderbach

Paulist Press
New York/Mahwah, NJ

The Scripture quotations contained herein are from the New Revised Standard Version: Catholic Edition Copyright © 1989 and 1993, by the Division of Christian Education of the National Council of the Churches of Christ in the United States of America. Used by permission. All rights reserved.

Cover and book design by Lynn Else

Library of Congress Cataloging-in-Publication Data

Liderbach, Daniel.
    The Jesus of history as the Christ of faith / Daniel Liderbach.
       p. cm.
    Includes bibliographical references and index.
    ISBN 978-0-8091-4542-3 (alk. paper)
    1. Jesus Christ—Historicity. 2. Jesus Christ—Biography—History and criticism. I. Title.
    BT303.2.L48 2009
    232.9'08—dc22

                                           2009004885

Published by Paulist Press
997 Macarthur Boulevard
Mahwah, New Jersey 07430

www.paulistpress.com

Printed and bound in the
United States of America

CONTENTS

Dedicated to
Madeline and Del Ray Rosson
and their children,
Ray, Rob, Maria, Rick, and Denine

I   Identifying the Jesus of History with the Christ of Faith

Rudolf Bultmann and the Problem

Rudolf Bultmann was a German army chaplain for evangelical soldiers during the First World War. He claimed to have discovered that the soldiers had been unwilling to accept the narrations of the words and deeds of Jesus in the New Testament. Thus, he chose to interpret the narrations of those words and deeds by using *form criticism*. Form criticism intended to situate each passage of the Bible within its original context. Bultmann exhaustively researched the narrations of Jesus and demonstrated that they had been imaginatively derived from specific Old Testament passages, specific teachings of first-century Judaism, or specific teachings of first-century Christianity. He inferred that almost none of the words and deeds of Jesus could be derived from that which Jesus had actually said or done.

Consequently, he set out to "demythologize" the New Testament and to lay aside that which he identified as the myths that were imaginative interpretations of the New Testament narrations of Jesus' revelations of the mystery of the God of Jesus Christ. Bultmann proposed that, in place of those revelations, the soldiers and other secularized Christians would be able to accept the authentic concerns that had been identified by the twentieth-century, German existentialist-philosopher Martin Heidegger (1889–1976).

Then in his watershed essay, "New Testament and Mythology: The Problem of Demythologizing the New Testament Proclamation" (1941), Bultmann acknowledged New Testament faith in Christ as "obedient surrender to God and as inner freedom from the world."[1]

One might note that faith in Christ for Bultmann is a surrender to *God*, not to the Jesus who is accessible to history's methods of textual inter- pretations of scripture, that is, New Testament hermeneutics. Although one may indeed sympathize with Bultmann's concern to revise the understanding of Christian faith so that twentieth-century believers might genuinely confess belief, one may also criticize him for assum- ing an improper point of departure. One may insist that the perspec- tive of the data of the New Testament is what the scriptural authors had striven to present.

Rudolf Bultmann began his reinterpretation of the New Testament's meaning of Christ by revising the theology of Paul, the first and perhaps most influential author in the New Testament. Bultmann assumed that Paul's formulation of the meaning of Christ had *become* the meaning of Christ for all subsequent authors of the Christian books. Thus, Bultmann researched Paul's formulation of the meaning of Christ as Lord. The question for that research was whether Paul would have acknowledged the historical Jesus as the Lord and Messiah. Bultmann responded for Paul by gratuitously asserting that, when Paul described Jesus Christ as teacher, exemplar, hero, and savior, he had not appealed to the earthly Jesus, but only to his own experience of Christ as the exalted Lord. Bultmann then asserted that Christ could be teacher and those other great roles only for those for whom he is already the Lord. Such believ- ers would confess the Christ as Lord, not because of the deeds of the long-dead Jesus of history, but only because of the Christ of faith encountered in the church's preaching about the Christ.

Bultmann further centered upon the Christ of faith—that is, the church's preached Christ, not the Jesus of history—as the one who is still present for believers. The wondrous actions of the Jesus of history can be relevant, Bultmann argued, only in so far as they are a part of the church's preaching regarding the Christ of faith.[2]

Bultmann formulated that distinction in 1966 in his effort to dis- cern the meaning in Paul's writings concerning the Christ of faith. Post- Bultmannians, however, have generalized that distinction in this manner: the Jesus of history is distinct from the Christ of faith. They assumed that the Jesus of history is publicly accessible by historical methods of investigation. The Christ of faith, however, is privately accessible only by personal risk of commitment to him and his salva- tion. Furthermore, one risks such a commitment not because of the publicly verified actions or deeds of the Jesus of history, but because of one's personal response to the church's efforts to preaching motivating images about Christ.

Consequently, there is now an agreement among many New Testament scholars that the identity of the Christ of faith emerged from the believing community. The first-century community of believers confessed Christ as redeemer and savior and, therefore, began to fashion titles for and characteristics of Jesus—"Savior," "Redeemer," "Son of God"—in order to raise him above the human level and to identify the Christ of faith as the one in whom they as well as future believers could trust absolutely.

The Jesus Seminar and a Revision

Rudolf Bultmann's skepticism regarding the Jesus of history reigned until the 1950s when Ernst Käesemann and other students of Bultmann parted ways with him by denying his claim that form criticism had made impossible the search for the historical Jesus. They once more searched for the historical Jesus. However, that search faltered due to the skepticism of the theologians of the late twentieth century.

Then, late in the twentieth century, Robert W. Funk led a few dozen New Testament scholars in the *Jesus Seminar* to forge yet another path away from that which Bultmann had so convincingly laid out and which the historians' skepticism had confirmed. Funk formed the seminar to commence "the new quest for the historical Jesus," which asks who the Jesus of history is and whether the Jesus of history had asked his followers to risk committing themselves to him and to his salvation.

In their effort to justify their new search for the historical Jesus and the method of that search, the members of the Jesus Seminar fashioned new criteria for identifying the genuine words and deeds of the Jesus of history. Using these criteria to investigate the degree to which the Jesus of history had indeed presented himself as the one who became the Christ of faith, they asked whether the community of believers formulated the identity of the Christ of faith, not because of those who fashioned the preaching, as Bultmann suggested, but because of Jesus' self-revelation in history.

Method of Approaching the Jesus of History

The new quest for the historical Jesus is indeed a historical quest. The Jesus Seminar identified a historical method comprised of new criteria with which it would struggle to discern the genuine words and deeds of the Jesus of history.

The seminar's method acknowledges that the gospels' literature regarding the sayings and deeds of Jesus was created by the church in order to express and to serve faith concerns. However, it also acknowledges that there is a historical basis upon which the New Testament authors grounded their confessional concerns. The seminar's method uncovers that historical basis.

Criteria of the Seminar's Methodology

The criterion of *discontinuity* identifies New Testament passages that are in continuity with themes neither of the Hebrew Scriptures (Old Testament) nor of the early church. Such discontinuous New Testament passages are assumed to have emerged from the genuine sayings or actions of Jesus. Any of the features of the sayings or deeds that are both present in and yet relatively distinct from the concerns of the church's preaching about Jesus, for example, preaching about his acceptance of being baptized by John, are very likely to be genuine deeds or sayings, to reflect the original impact of Jesus on some or several of his first disciples, even though those passages are discontinuous with the church concerns with preaching its themes about Jesus.[3]

Such words or deeds, attributed to Jesus and presented as discontinuous with the Judaism of the time or with the early church's confession of the Christ of faith, have a good claim to have as their source the genuine acts or sayings of Jesus. Moreover, the less closely a saying or motif is present in the Jewish tradition or the tradition of the Christ of faith, the more likely that it goes back to Jesus himself. An example of such discontinuity is Jesus' sweeping prohibition of all oaths (Matt 5:34, 37). Oaths had been a common practice among Jews and a tolerated practice in the early church. Nonetheless, the New Testament portrayed Jesus as having condemned all oaths, though that condemnation was in discontinuity with both the Jewish and the early church traditions.

Some of that discontinuous material even runs counter both to the Judaism of Jesus' time and to the certainly ascertained preaching of the church. Such passages appeared to the Jesus Seminar to be embarrassing to the church. Why would the early church have created New Testament passages that run counter to its preached theology and consequently embarrass the church? By the criterion of *embarrassment*, the Jesus Seminar concluded that such materials did not have as their source the early church's creative expression of its theology and faith. Using this method, the seminar concluded, rather, that such material had been preserved and recorded as the remembered sayings or deeds of Jesus. Because that source provides the genuine data regarding Jesus, some material was preserved by the evangelists in spite of its making the church's preaching and theology more difficult.[4]

That criterion of embarrassment also directed the Jesus Seminar to discern the genuine occurrences of Jesus in history. It led those scripture scholars to ask whether the proclaimed occurrences support the first Christ of faith data that the church had established, whether they might support the Judaism contemporary with Jesus, or whether they support the preaching of the early church. Such embarrassing passages became more important to the Jesus Seminar if they appeared in more than one of the four earliest sources of Jesus data.

Two examples are Jesus' prohibiting every form of divorce in Mark 10:2–12 and the woman from Syrophoenicia outmaneuvering Jesus into curing her daughter in Mark 7:25–30. Such words or deeds of Jesus that would have embarrassed the early church would hardly have their source in it. The church would not have gone out of its way to create material that only embarrassed its Lord or that weakened its position in arguments with its opponents. So the Jesus Seminar inferred that the genuine source of such actions or sayings is Jesus himself.

There are not four but six possible "gospel" sources for any cited words or deeds of Jesus. The first Gospel was written by Mark, perhaps in the year 80 CE, and is one such source. There also probably was a number of remembered and perhaps written sayings of Jesus; some of them were collected in a not-as-yet-discovered source that is known as *die Quelle* (the source) or *Q*. This is the second source. In perhaps 90 CE, Matthew and Luke copied from Mark and from Q to fashion their Gospels. Matthew and Luke comprise a third source. The Gospel of John, written near the end of the first century, appears to be quite independent of those three sources. John is the fourth source. Paul, who wrote just one generation after Jesus' death, is a fifth source of the words and actions of Jesus. The Gospel of Thomas is the sixth.

Occurrences that are found in more than one and especially in three or four sources are also considered to be genuine.[5] There are not a great many such passages. Some events and sayings are recognized by all five sources, for example, the Farewell Meal. Such *multiple attestations* of sayings or actions are assumed to be material that the author preserved because they are genuine sayings or actions of Jesus. Thus, if a saying or action attributed to Jesus fits any of those criteria—discontinuity, embarrassment, or multiple attestation—and especially if it fits more than one, then it can be considered to be quite likely genuine.[6]

Next, there are in the Gospels other sayings or deeds of Jesus that fit in well with the Jesus of history data that can be established by the above three criteria of the seminar's method. Such sayings or deeds have a good chance of being genuinely historical, for example, disputes with adversaries over legal observance.[7] One could dismiss such data only riskingly: it has the support of the already-established data, which represent the criterion of coherence.

Finally, there is the criterion of Jesus' *rejection and execution*. There is universal agreement that Jesus was arrested, indicted, convicted, and crucified by the Roman procurator. Some words or deeds of Jesus appear to have led to his violent rejection by the Jewish and Roman officials. Jesus would not have been executed if he were simply a man who told parables or a bland poet who directed people to live in trust. He must have confronted political and religious values in disturbing and infuriating manners. Gospel words and deeds of Jesus that portray him so are likely genuine,[8] even though they may be contrary to the Jesus-image that has become conventional—the compassionate healer. Jesus must have been an individual who confronted others with his demand that they change because of his proclamation. Moreover, because he had no officially recognized right do so, his confrontational sayings and deeds would have grievously offended the Jewish and Roman authorities.

The Jesus Seminar's methods have also discerned a development in the Synoptic tradition's gathering and ordering of the Jesus tradition that had already been in at least oral circulation within the community. For example, the Evangelists Mark, Matthew, and Luke exercised increasing independence in their ordering of that material. As a result, we in the twenty-first century must give up hope of identifying anything like a historical order in the recorded sayings and deeds of Jesus. Nonetheless, by using a method such as that which the seminar has formulated, one can identify some actions and words that are more likely to be genuine.

The Jesus of History and the Historical Jesus

The seminar's method of access to the historical Jesus is limited by what it is capable of accessing. It attends only to those passages written by church members that were either discontinuous with contemporary Judaism or church culture, were embarrassing to the church, or were attested in more than one of the five early sources for the historical Jesus. Such passages give access to a historical individual known as Jesus of Nazareth. However, they do not give access to the unique individual characteristics of the Jesus of history. The Jesus of history was the individual who had a unique physical appearance and who acted and responded with unique self-expressions. Nothing regarding his physical appearance and only some of those self-expressions have survived. Therefore, we do not have access to the Jesus of history. A small number of the actions and the teachings of the historical Jesus are all that remain of that Jesus. Those remembered glimpses provide access to the limited characteristics of the Jesus whom we think of as the historical Jesus. However, the Jesus of history, that is, the individual in his entirety, was not recorded and therefore not remembered. Consequently, that Jesus is not accessible to those who live in the twenty-first century.[9] Those who have an interest in the Jesus of history and who live in the twenty-first century have a choice to make. If they have interest only in the Jesus of history, then they might turn their backs on the method of the Jesus Seminar because it does not offer to them the Jesus whom they desire to know. However, if they have an interest in any historical characteristics that a historical method may discern in Jesus, then they might welcome the seminar's method.

Those who fashioned the historical method of the seminar intended to discern those characteristics about Jesus that were remembered, that is, Jesus' actions and sayings that made a memorable impact upon his disciples. Thus, the method presents not the Jesus of history but the perceived and remembered historical Jesus.[10] There is no other historical Jesus available to those who are removed from Jesus by almost two millennia. One may want to ask some questions about Jesus, but which answers have not been remembered. For example, one may want to know whether Jesus was literate, how he interrelated with boyhood friends, or whether he was graceful in interacting with females. Yet that information has not been remembered. As a result, one has access only to the remembered, historical Jesus, not to the Jesus of history.

The people of the twenty-first century therefore have access to the historical Jesus just as they have access to anyone about whom something was written in ancient times. In almost all cases, ancient writings present, not how an individual's character may have developed over time, but rather the remembered episodes and sayings that document the historical person. Apparently those episodes and sayings drew the interest of certain people who formulated, collected, and recounted them into remembered formats. Eventually those formats regarding the historical Jesus entered into the material that now partially comprises the Gospels.[11]

Unfortunately, other material that may be interesting to people today is simply no longer available. One cannot know that which was neither remembered nor recorded about an individual who lived thousands of years ago.

In addition, the remembered material about Jesus was written from the perspective, not of the objective historian, but of those who were concerned with promoting faith in Christ. That faith affected the entire narrative about Jesus from beginning to end. When one acknowledges that all of the written memories were recounted from the perspective of faith, then one must also acknowledge the limited scope of its interest in the Jesus of history and therefore the limited scope of the identity of the historical Jesus who is accessible now.[12] Nonetheless, it will satisfy anyone who now has interest in knowing how those with faith remembered Jesus.

Still, the twenty-first-century individual can rightly assume certain things: the Jesus of history was a first-century Jew who operated in a first-century milieu. He was brought up as a religious Jew who learned the Hebrew Scriptures in a synagogue class reading those scriptures. He carried out his ministry within the land of Israel. There is no historical dispute over his historical execution on the charge of being a messianic pretender ("King of the Jews").[13] Thus, one does have access to some historical data that complements faith's remembered data regarding the Jesus of history.

II Proclaimer of the Kingdom of God

"Jesus was a magician who used his magic as a ladder to claim to be 'son of God.'" That has been the belief of a number of New Testament scholars, such as Morton Smith.[1] However, others have insisted that Jesus' mighty acts meant something far different from magic to many of those who witnessed them. For instance, the Beelzebub controversy (Mark 3:22–30) indicates that Jesus' miraculous signs divided witnesses into followers who confessed the presence of the divine in Jesus and into skeptics who perceived the power of Beelzebub.[2]

There is a great deal of evidence in the gospels that many who witnessed Jesus' miracles concluded that he was a prophet, who spoke of the gradual unfolding of God's revelation. Yet there seems to have been some who dismissed Jesus as no more than a minor religious voice. Nonetheless, the great majority of New Testament scholars—note the evidence even here of the criterion of multiple attestation—judge that Jesus himself had claimed to be the herald who inaugurated the in-breaking of God into history, the prophet who insisted that "the kingdom of God is in your midst," and the thaumaturge, or miracle worker, who performed signs that the Kingdom was indeed giving evidence of its presence among humans.[3]

The central theme of the ministry of Jesus the prophet was his proclamation of the Kingdom of God. Many scholars—for example, Joachim Jeremias, Norman Perrin, John Meier—insist upon that theme. The Jesus Seminar agrees as well, on the basis of its methodological criteria. Jesus presented himself as the proclaimer of the Kingdom of God.

By the criterion of discontinuity the Jesus Seminar has directed attention to the fact that the phrase *Kingdom of God* does not occur in the

Hebrew Scriptures and occurs rarely in the ancient Hebrew religious books not identified as the Hebrew Scriptures, that is, the Apocrypha. *The Kingdom of God* is mentioned, for example, in the Wisdom of Solomon (10:10). In the New Testament the term is not common apart from the Gospels. This seems to suggest that it was a genuine saying, that Jesus had not taken it from the Jewish tradition, and that the Christian tradition which came after him had not gradually allowed it to slip into disuse.[4] Yet the term is repeatedly on the lips of Jesus in the Gospels.

The Kingdom of God denotes that God reigns over a territory that extends as far in space as creation, as far in time as human history. Jesus proclaimed that God is in a dynamic relation to all those in creation, to all those in history, rather than only to those within a delimited territory.[5]

However, one may argue that the symbolic meaning of Jesus' Kingdom of God connotes a wider range of meanings. Jesus' symbol can be compared to Michelangelo's symbol of a pietà. Michelangelo had completed three pietà sculptures (the first is the *Pietà* best known by all) and had been working on his fourth when he died. The sculptor had been attempting to unfold the depths of meaning that the symbol held for him. So, too, Jesus' proclamation attempted to unfold, for example, through the parables, the many depths of meaning of the Kingdom of God he envisioned.[6]

Very many of the gospel parables begin with the words "The kingdom of God is like...." Though form criticism has judged most of the words put into the mouth of Jesus to be inauthentic, it has considered the parables genuine sayings of Jesus. In them Jesus purposely made the symbol of the Kingdom a central part of his proclamation.[7]

In addition the Beatitudes (Matt 5:3–12 and Luke 6:20–23) are proclamations by Jesus, the eschatological prophet, that with the already-present Kingdom of God, one can expect the not-yet-fully-present Kingdom to invert all meanings.[8] Eschatology is understood to be that which is already present, though not yet fully present. As the Kingdom unfolds in history step-by-step, it increasingly transforms all.

Jesus' Proclamation of the Mystery

Jesus' proclamation of the Kingdom of God as already present and "at hand" had challenged his hearers to trust in the mystery of that

Kingdom, to trust that the God of Jesus Christ, or the Presence, was "at hand" and active in the midst of the human community. This Kingdom of God was not a demonstration of force, nor of vindication, nor of vengeance against Rome. Rather, Jesus' proclamation called for its hearers to give up any prior agendas and expectations as they trusted in the divine Presence who works hiddenly and enigmatically here, now.[9]

The Jews to whom Jesus addressed his proclamation had been living in the hope that God would return in power to dwell in the Temple and would reestablish the power of the Davidic dynasty. Hearers *today* live in the hope that God—the Presence—will actively provide what they desire or need. To hearers both ancient and present, Jesus proclaimed that the Presence is already actively, yet mysteriously working to achieve good, even if that good may not be what hearers assume that they desire or need.

In fact, the good that the Presence is achieving in the human community may be wholly other and unexpected. Examples of such unexpected good are found in Jesus' parables. Jesus proclaimed the parable of the tares that the Son of Man will send his angels to gather all at the close of the age (Matt 13:40–42). Similarly Jesus proclaimed the great net cast into the sea; the net gathered fish of every kind, which the men then sorted as good to be saved and bad to be thrown out (Matt 13:47–50). Again, Jesus proclaimed his vision of the end-time, the little apocalypse, and that his hearers were to expect many figures to come in order to lead them astray (the signs of the Kingdom remain enigmatic); yet his hearers were to endure to the end as the Presence hiddenly does good (Matt 24:3–13). So, too, the appearance of the Son of Man would be completely different from his expected *enigmatic* appearance (Matt 24:30–31). Finally, Jesus proclaimed the mysterious presence of the Son of Man within the human community "to the end of the age" (Matt 28:20).[10] Such parables proclaimed that the Presence indeed worked and works among us, even if the Presence does not work in that manner we may desire and long for the divine One to act.

After the resurrection, therefore, the disciples expected something from their Lord, although not that he would return leading a heavenly army or a host of angels. Rather, Jesus the proclaimer had led them to expect that the Risen One would accomplish some wondrous event that would so transform the world that the traditional forms of

Judaism and the power of arms would no longer be needed. So they must have learned, perhaps from the Risen One, that they were to expect the Presence to act in their midst, but in a manner wholly beyond human imagining. Neither the disciples nor the Jerusalem aristocracy, that is, the Sadducees, nor the Romans would have been capable of imagining the wonder that the Risen One would achieve in the community.[11] Yet the disciples had maintained hope in the great deed of the Risen One because of the message that Jesus had passed to them.

Mark's portrayal of the Farewell Meal included Jesus' proclamation that he would "never again drink of the fruit of the vine until that day when I drink it new in the kingdom of God" (Mark 14:25). In that verse, Mark portrayed Jesus as foretelling his own death. However, Jesus also promised that his cause—inaugurating the Kingdom of God—is the cause of the Presence. Additionally, Jesus promised that the Presence would vindicate Jesus' cause and prophecy by bringing about the Kingdom and by seating Jesus at the banquet in the Kingdom. Mark thus wrote a call of hope and trust in the Presence who will make the mystery of the Kingdom come even in the face of the death of Jesus.[12]

The disciples might still have desired that the Presence would work vengeance upon those responsible for Jesus' death. Yet they were challenged, as we now are challenged, to trust that the good of the Presence is better than the good that humans desire.

The proclamation of the Kingdom of God—the Presence dwelling among humans and acting there—identifies the Kingdom as a gratuitous gift to all. Because the Presence is freely there for all, all are summoned by the Presence to acknowledge the Presence and to respond as they are invited. To acknowledge the nonsensuous Presence and to respond to the nonempirical summons and the mysterious Kingdom is to become childlike in one's innocence and trust.[13] Those who on the contrary insist upon logical or empirical demonstration of the Kingdom refuse to be childlike and thus inhibit themselves from engaging with the Kingdom of God.

Furthermore, Jesus is portrayed by Mark and Matthew as having insisted that the Kingdom of God includes sinners (Mark 2:17, Matt 10:6, Matt 15:24). The Jesus Seminar's criterion of embarrassment insists that the inclusion of sinners is a genuine saying of Jesus: neither the Jewish tradition nor the church would have created such a saying

since both urged believers to put sin aside. Worse, Jesus was also portrayed as having accepted those sinners who were tax collectors, that
is, agents of organized crime who transgressed the pharisaic purity
code and collaborated with Rome's occupation of Israel (Matt
9:9–13).[14] The Presence's gratuitous embrace includes not only those
who strive to be morally good, but also those who find themselves
identified as morally sinful.

The parable of the banquet, which apparently was in Q (Matt
22:1–10 and Luke 14:15–24), acknowledged that many of those who
had first been invited, that is, those morally good, had refused to accept
their invitations. So the king who had prepared the banquet sent his
servants to the thoroughfares and directed them to invite all whom they
found there, that is, to invite the bad as well as the good to the banquet.[15] The parable suggests that the Kingdom of God can too-readily be
rejected by those who consider themselves to be righteous, while those
who acknowledged themselves to be so flawed as to need the Presence
are ready and willing to accept and to confess the Kingdom.

Matthew portrayed Jesus as summoning sinners to the banquet of
the Kingdom without asking sinners to repent before responding. Jesus
thus appears to have been one who is a friend of those people who
remain sinners indefinitely. For example, the portrait of the apostle Levi
(Matt 9:9–13) includes no summons to Levi to repent of being a tax collector. That portrait implies that Jesus proclaimed the Kingdom of God
as present unconditionally, that is, as a gratuitous gift, even to those who
did not observe the many hundreds of regulations that were derived
from the Mosaic code. The Kingdom was present to those who lived outside the Law, to tax collectors and to prostitutes (Matt 21:31), as a gift to
them as well, even without the condition that they turn from sin.[16] That
image of the Jesus of history powerfully suggests one of the causes that
led his followers to identify him as the Christ of faith. Jesus had reinterpreted the Presence in a most positive and approachable manner. Those
who had been formed with the need to observe the Law strictly must
have preferred the tolerant God proclaimed by Jesus to the righteous
God proclaimed by the high priests. So the common Jews who listened
to Jesus would likely have concluded that he was the prophet of the
Presence, was even the representative of the Presence. Jesus' willingness
to include even those who had been rejected as wicked, that is, his insistence that the Presence embraces tax collectors and prostitutes, held out

the hope to all Israel that all were in the Kingdom of God, that no moral or legal failure severed one from the Presence.

Even the truly wicked—those who had implicitly or explicitly rejected the commandments of the Law—were welcome into the Kingdom proclaimed by Jesus. That was most attractive to the Jews, though it made Jesus' message most offensive to normal Jewish piety.[17] The faithful observance of the Jewish Law required a degree of financial success; thus, a significant number of Jews were too poor to observe the Law. Yet all not welcome to worship in the Temple of Solomon were included in the Kingdom of God as preached by Jesus. He thus presented himself as the one who had been promised by the prophets.

The Eschatology of the Kingdom of God

Jesus proclaimed the Kingdom of God as already present in his ministry, but as in tension with the not-as-yet-fully and finally emergent Kingdom. That tension is eschatology. Because Jesus identified the Kingdom as having such tension, his vision of the Kingdom was eschatological. The not-yet-full and final Kingdom will reveal itself in a fullness of power that is present, but not yet fully in the already-here Kingdom.[18]

The already-present Kingdom was described in the Gospel of Luke as "for in fact the kingdom of God is among you" (Luke 17:20–21). Neither Mark nor Matthew has a parallel proclamation; however, both usually portrayed Jesus as proclaiming that the Kingdom is in the future. Because of the discontinuity of Luke's statement with the customary statements about the Kingdom, John P. Meier judged that "the kingdom of God is in your midst" expresses the authentic words of Jesus.[19] If that is a correct judgment, then Jesus is to be understood as having insisted that the Kingdom of God is indeed now at hand, a source of hope for all the living.

There are a number of New Testament sayings that identify the Kingdom as in the future (Luke 7:28), as well as in the present (Luke 17:20). Jesus' Kingdom sayings from the Lord's Prayer, "Your kingdom come" (Matt 6:10); from the Farewell Meal, "I will never again drink…until that day when I drink it new in the kingdom of God" (Mark 14:25); from the vision of the Gentiles' joining with the Jews in the Kingdom's banquet (Matt 8:11–12); from the Beatitudes of the Sermon on the Mount (Matt 5:2–12); and from his sayings that limit the time before the Kingdom's arrival (Mark 13:30)—all these suggest that Jesus understood the Kingdom as future.[20]

Jesus thought that the power of God was simultaneously present at work in the world, though the time would come when all opposing powers would be eliminated.[21] Many people in Israel apparently responded to such a vision of hope by acknowledging Jesus as the prophet who spoke as no one previously had spoken. He appeared, therefore, to them to be the promised one, the Messiah, the Christ of faith.

Furthermore, the people of Israel understood Jesus to have proclaimed that the Kingdom of God was climactic, that is, that it would bring to fulfillment the history of Israel. However, they also understood his vision of the Kingdom to be transforming. With the Kingdom, everything is changed: divorce is abolished; vengeance, outlawed; wealth, power, and false piety, devalued. Anyone who was willing to affirm unconditional love of and trust in the Presence as the first commandment was "not far from the kingdom of God" (Mark 12:34), that is, was already nearly living in the Kingdom of God.[22] Those who felt the dynamism of that vision of Jesus apparently took the next step of proclaiming him to be the Christ, the one in whom Israel was to trust.

Liberation of the Jews from the Law

Multiple attestation—four gospel sources—confirms that Jesus' "cleansing of the Temple" was a genuine act of Jesus. That act demonstrated Jesus' self-understanding that the power of the Presence, that is, the power of the present Kingdom of God, was active in him, that he was the prophet and agent of the Presence, and that he was the replacement of the Temple: "See, something greater than Solomon is here" (Luke 11:31).[23]

Those Jews contemporaneous with Jesus had learned from the high priests that they were obliged to follow the dictates of Temple worship, as well as all other prescriptions of the Law. However, Jesus' action—the cleansing of the Temple—challenged the Jews to consider themselves liberated from prescriptions of the Law and able to trust in their freedom. Those who chose to follow Jesus in such a reinterpretation were in effect choosing to accept Jesus as the unique prophet, as the Promised One, as the Christ.

The exorcisms—multiple attestation supports them as genuine acts of Jesus—were interpreted by the evangelists as signs that the power of the Kingdom of God, namely, the Presence, was actively at work in the ministry of Jesus. So, too, Jesus' forgiving sins was his claim to be capable of doing that which the prophets had announced that the Promised One would do.[24] Those Jews who chose to follow Jesus risked acknowledging him to be the Christ, the one who uniquely could interpret for them what the Presence asks of humans.

The healing signs by Jesus—signs that the Presence was forcefully at work in his ministry—attracted crowds and special close followers. They had chosen to accept the proclamation by Jesus that the Kingdom of God was eschatological, that is, was already present among them, though it was not yet fully as present as it would be.[25] One can easily imagine that witnesses of Jesus' healings would have felt challenged to respond most trustingly or most hostilely. The line had been drawn between those who acknowledged Jesus to be the promised Christ and those who rejected him as a very clever imposter.

Salvation for All

Matthew portrayed Jesus as having promised salvation for all peoples, not only for the Jews: "Many will come from east and west and will eat with Abraham and Isaac and Jacob in the kingdom of heaven, while the heirs of the kingdom will be thrown into the outer darkness" (Matt 8:11–12). Jesus' having reached out to tax collectors, prostitutes, and sinners was an embarrassing action that demonstrated his conviction of the vision behind those words.[26] Sinners who responded to Jesus' invitation and nonsinners who joined in table fellowship with him were in effect acknowledging Jesus as capable of reinterpreting the Presence for them.

However, there were others who rejected Jesus as unqualified to reinterpret the Presence. They accused him of representing Beelzebub (Luke 11:18). In response to them, Jesus identified himself with "the finger of God," that is, with the power of the Kingdom of God upon earth. The Presence was already reaching, touching, and transforming the lives of certain people on earth even then.[27] If, as the Jesus Seminar insists, those words of Jesus are authentic, then the evangelists remembered many Jews as accepting Jesus as much more than a human—in fact as the Promised One, the Christ.

Jesus' Challenge: Stop, Turn Around, Acknowledge the Kingdom

Jesus' proclamation of the Kingdom of God was a challenge to his hearers to change their disposition to the whole of life. The word *repentance* was used to translate that change. The meaning of *repentance* is critical in the interpretation of the response that Jesus invited. *To repent* means to stop, to turn around, and to acknowledge what one had not noticed. In the case of Jesus' proclamation, to repent is to acknowledge that the Kingdom is already present in all of life. Because the Kingdom is present everywhere, a new disposition toward experience is the challenge before all those who were or are hearers of the proclamation.

Jesus provided a few examples of that new disposition. Apparently, he had insisted upon a new attitude toward marriage: divorce was no longer tolerable. Also, he proclaimed a new way of looking on material things: sell one's possessions, give alms, and provide oneself only with heaven's treasures. Furthermore, Jesus proclaimed that the Kingdom inverts the social values of conventional wisdom: anyone who would be first must be the last of all and the servant of all.[28] Those examples of repentance because of the Kingdom are characteristic of the radically new disposition with which believers are to approach the Presence in life. Because the Kingdom is present in every experience, the believer is challenged to address each experience with a disposition quite different from the one that many follow conventionally.

The Jews had presumed that, when the Promised One came, he would reestablish the Kingdom of David—a political and military power on earth. Jesus unexpectedly proclaimed that the presence of the Kingdom required the Jews to reinterpret the meaning of the Promised One. Jesus insisted that he had come not to bring the peace of a military power on earth, but a sword that would divide believers from the earth's powers (Matt 10:34, Luke 12:51). He inverted the meaning of the Promised One in the Kingdom: Christ is not the source of soft comfort, but a point of division, forcing hearers to decide for or against the reign of the Presence.

The disciples, too, would be a point of division. Jesus heralded that their proclamation of the reign of the Presence would not unite all towns, but divide those towns accepting the Kingdom from those rejecting it (Matt 10:12–15). The Kingdom was to divide hearers from the earth's powers, not to unite them. Jesus' proclamation confronted his hearers with a crisis of decision.

For instance, the question of whether his disciples ought to fast drew from Jesus the challenge to believe that he had proclaimed something so transforming—the Kingdom of God as now present—that one could not respond by fasting. Mark envisioned that Kingdom as a wedding feast (Mark 2:18–20); wedding guests cannot fast as long as the bridegroom is with them.[29] The analogy is that hearers are to respond to the proclamation that the Presence is active on earth in joy and in festivity, not in self-denial.

The Matthean and Lucan traditions of the Lord's Prayer, though they differ in wording, agree that Jesus taught his disciples to pray that the Kingdom will come, as it has "not yet fully" come. This eschatological fulfillment of the Kingdom calls for a change from conventional dispositions by relying on the will of the Presence, not on self; hallowing the name of the Presence, not the word of the Hebrew Scriptures; praising the name of the Presence, rather than worshipping in cultic sacrifices; spontaneously following one's new heart and new spirit, rather than criticizing self for sins.[30] Indeed Jesus confronted his hearers with the need to choose whether or not to adopt an entirely new mindset because of the Kingdom of the Presence.

Perhaps the gravest challenge of Jesus' proclamation of the Kingdom of God is his radical identity of the Presence as *Abba*—the first Aramaic word that an infant used to address its father. The word is translated by terms such as "Da Da" or "Pa Pa," that is, words of intimacy, love, compassion, tolerance, and understanding.[31] Jesus challenged and challenges his hearers to put aside the conventional vision of the Presence as a judge and to adopt his radically new vision of the Presence as a parent who immediately and intimately loves each individual. That can be a most optimistic vision to adopt. One can adopt it, however, only if one is willing to break with the conventional vision. Such a break requires one to live in crisis.

III The Sayings of Jesus

This book searches to discover how the new quest for the historical Jesus has argued that the Jesus of history identified himself as the Christ of faith. Certainly, the quest's identification of the genuine sayings of Jesus is most relevant. The important question regarding any genuine saying of Jesus is whether it indicates that Jesus identified himself as the Christ, as the Promised One, as the Messiah. An alternative question is whether the hearers of Jesus' sayings during his life had understood him to be the Christ, the Messiah.

The Criteria for Genuine Sayings of Jesus

A further criterion—a criterion that expands the criterion of discontinuity identified in the second chapter—emerges in the search to identify genuine sayings of Jesus: double dissimilarity. There are New Testament sayings that cannot be accounted for as traditional Jewish material but as dissimilar from such data. That is one dissimilarity. Neither can some of these sayings be accounted for as later church material but are also dissimilar from that data. That is the double dissimilarity. Sayings that have the characteristic of such double dissimilarity can, as the Jesus Seminar claimed, be "safely" attributed to Jesus. It is assumed that sayings that reflect traditional Jewish material or traditional church material emerged not from Jesus but from the Jewish or the Christian tradition. However, sayings that can be traced back to neither source can be assumed to have emerged from Jesus himself.[1]

That criterion profitably takes its place, along with the discriminating criteria of discontinuity, embarrassment, and multiple attestation, as an indicator of expressions that can be identified as having their source in genuine sayings of Jesus.

One should bear in mind that, although genuine sayings by Jesus had as their context first-century Judaism, they led to the movement of believers who eventually broke with Judaism. The student does well to conclude that there is a substantial coherence among what Jesus intended to say, what he saw as his relationship to his nation's goals and religion, and what led to his death and ultimately to the Christian movement.[2] That hypothesis would lead the student to conclude that the meanings of the sayings that the evangelists articulated were the same as the meanings of the sayings that Jesus had expressed.

Jesus' native tongue, Aramaic, formed his way of expressing himself. As anyone who has even briefly studied philology knows, one's mother tongue forms one's manner of perceiving experience. Aramaic had, of course, a number of characteristic forms of expression, such as the paradoxical reversals in the aphorisms of the Beatitudes: "Blessed are those who mourn; they shall be comforted." The paradox is that those who mourn will find that their mourning turns to comfort. Also, there is the saying that one who loves his life will lose it, while the one who hates his life will keep it. Jesus' Aramaic influence emerges in the Gospels' many paradoxical reversals in the sayings of Jesus.[3] Such paradoxical aphorisms can thus be regarded as having their source in the Aramaic language of Jesus rather than in the Greek language, the language used by the New Testament authors.

Another typical Aramaic form of aphorism is the inversion within a complex sentence. An example: "If any want to become my followers, let them deny themselves and take up their cross and follow me" (Mark 8:34). Again, the form of that inversion is not typical Greek, but rather Aramaic.[4] Therefore, such inversions are more likely to be the genuine words of Jesus. However, other criteria need to be used in order to confirm that hypothesis. Such Aramaic paradoxical inversions are found in many of the Jesus sayings in the New Testament. If other criteria—such as multiple attestation—indicate that those are genuine words of Jesus, then one can safely conclude that Jesus spoke them.[5]

An increasing knowledge of the characteristics of Aramaic has led to these more-educated hypotheses regarding those kinds of self-expression that Jesus would have spoken.

Jesus' Challenge to Unique Sacrifice

Not all of the New Testament "Jesus sayings" can be traced to Aramaic forms of self-expression. Some sayings, although not identifiable as having Aramaic forms, still meet the criterion of being discontinuous. For example, Jesus' saying in Matthew 10:37, "Whoever loves father or mother more than me is not worthy of me," is shockingly discontinuous with both first-century Jewish and Christian culture. In the first-century Mediterranean world, Jews and Christians found their identities in their extended families. The quoted saying, though not in an identifiable Aramaic form, is so discontinuous that it most likely had Jesus as its source.[6] Our increasing knowledge of first-century Near East cultures provides further linguistic assistance in identifying the genuine sayings of Jesus.

Eschatological Sayings

If eschatology is defined as the tension between the "already present" and the "not yet fully present," then there are New Testament sayings regarding the Kingdom of God that are eschatological expressions. For example, Romans 8:22–24 cites such eschatology:

> We know that the whole creation has been groaning in labor pains until now; and not only the creation, but we ourselves, who have the first fruits of the Spirit, groan inwardly while we wait for adoption, the redemption of our bodies. For in hope we were saved. Now hope that is seen is not hope. For who hopes for what is seen?

Paul envisioned the Presence as desiring to delay showing the divine wrath and power and consequently patiently enduring the "groans," that is, the complaints of humanity, even though humanity in Paul's judgment deserved destruction. Paul focused upon the tension between the already present experiences of the divine wrath (here the human guilt of either executing Jesus or of failing to strive to prevent that execution) and the not-yet-fully-present experience of the divine wrath and power of God (here the Presence's withholding punishment from those same guilty humans in the early church).

Similar eschatological "Kingdom sayings" are found in Matthew. Both Paul and Matthew have included sayings of Jesus that have him express words that present the eschatology of the Kingdom.

The authentic words of Jesus may also be simple riddles. Ben Meyer, in *The Aims of Jesus*, had concluded from his study of the words of Jesus that he often taught in riddles to challenge his hearers to reinterpret.[7] Thus, the study of the New Testament literature provides yet another criterion to identify the genuine sayings of Jesus.

Meyer identified many such riddles, for example, "No sign will be given to [this evil and adulterous generation] except for sign of the prophet Jonah" (Matt 12:39); or "We heard him say, 'I will destroy this temple that is made with hands, and in three days I will build another, not made with hands'" (Mark 14:58). By teaching in riddles, Jesus was leading his hearers to reinterpret how the Messiah, the Promised One, might fulfill the prophets' promises. The more dense of the riddles— for example, "Go tell that fox [Herod Antipas] for me, 'Listen, I am casting out demons and performing cures today and tomorrow, and on the third day I finish my work'" (Luke 13:32)[8]—clearly are attempts by Jesus to invite his hearers to completely reinterpret the meaning of the Promised One. Another example is that the expected Messiah was to be the new David, a military and political victor; but Jesus as the Promised One, the seemingly irrelevant individual from the backwaters of Galilee, claimed to be the new David. That riddle of Jesus suggested that he was indeed the Messiah as promised by the third of the three authors of the book of Isaiah (Isa 61:1, 2), but not the expected victorious new David. Rather, the riddle suggests without expressing it that Jesus was the expected Messiah—he drove out demons and healed, as Third Isaiah foresaw; however, his messianic career would be marked not by victory and power but by a termination.

Sayings That Cut Against the Social and Religious Grain

The evangelists have recorded sayings of Jesus that cut against the social and religious grain of both Judaism and early Christianity. One example is, "There is nothing outside a person that by going in can defile, but the things that come out are what defile" (Mark 7:15). Such a saying would have surprised and shocked the Jews and the early Jewish Christians, both of whom considered the dietary code of the Law to be a divine requirement. Another example is the "Good Samaritan" parable (Luke 10:30–35) that reversed the widely accepted evaluation of Jews and Samaritans—Jews as trustworthy, Samaritans as threats.[9] To have shocked the first-century Jews and Christians would have been counterproductive for the evangelists. They wrote in order to persuade first-century Jews and Greeks to believe in the God of Jesus Christ. Moreover, all of those Jews and many of those Greeks knew the Jewish prejudice against Samaritans. Regardless, such a shocking parable was recorded. The assumption is that it is a genuine parable told by Jesus.

Sayings That Refer to Jesus' Exorcisms and Cures

There were New Testament sayings that identified Jesus as one who had the divine power to perform exorcisms and cures. One such saying is Jesus' response to the claim that he used the power of Beelzebub to drive out demons. He explained the power that he exercised by claiming that "the finger of God" was active in his ministry (Matt 12:27).

Another instance was Jesus' sending out his disciples with authority to cast out demons, showing that he understood himself as one who had the power to give divine authority to those whom he chose (Mark 3:15).

A third example was the report of Jesus' response to the Baptist's query regarding his identity: "Go and tell John what you hear and see: the blind receive their sight, the lame walk, the lepers are cleansed, the deaf hear, the dead are raised, and the poor have good news brought to them" (Matt 11:5). In so citing the works that the third author of the Book of Isaiah had predicted that the Messiah would perform (Isa 61:1, 2), Jesus identified himself to be the Christ.

A final example is Jesus' refusal to respond to the demand that he provide a sign from heaven in order to justify his right to act for the Presence. "No sign will be given to this generation" (Mark 8:11) is an indication that Jesus understood himself to be the adequate sign that God had been working through him.[10]

Such sayings were maintained by the evangelists as indications that the Jesus of history understood himself to be more than simply a charismatic individual, more than the "wandering sage" that the Jesus Seminar identified him to be. Jesus presented himself in those sayings as the Christ, the Promised One, the Messiah.

Evangelists' "Revision" of Jesus' Proclamation

After Jesus' death, his followers retreated from the radical vision of his proclamation and represented their more modest "memories" of his vision. Using common Jewish lore, the Greek translation of the Hebrew Scriptures, the vision of John the Baptist, and their own emerging convictions about Jesus, the expected Messiah, the evangelists wove an imaginative theological construct about the identity of Jesus.[11]

Examples of an Evangelist's revision of Jesus' vision are Mark's words in the mouth of Jesus: "The wedding guests cannot fast while the bridegroom is with them. As long as they have the bridegroom with them, they cannot fast" (Mark 2:19). Those enigmatic words of Jesus had been toned down by Mark, who used them to defend the followers' failure to follow the dietary laws of the Jews.[12] That challenging expression may indeed have been genuine words of Jesus. However, their original meaning seems to have been lost in their being used to defend a refusal to fast. Probably Jesus' original meaning had been that the bridegroom's proclamation of the Kingdom of God transformed and transforms all conventional laws and values.

Several such words of Jesus appear to have been situated in contexts that permit the original meanings to have slipped away. "Let us go across to the other side" (Mark 4:35) now appears to be no more than a suggestion by Jesus that his band ought to cross a lake, though its original meaning was likely a challenge to live as people transformed by the Kingdom. Or, "The time is fulfilled, and the kingdom of God has come near; repent, and believe in the good news" (Mark 1:15) has lost the intimations of its pristine meaning, which was perhaps a demand that one regard all of life as having new meaning because of the Kingdom.[13]

Conversely, words borrowed from the fund of common lore or from the Greek translation of the Hebrew Scriptures are put on Jesus' lips. Mark also put words of Plutarch and Diogenes Laertius on the lips of Jesus: "Those who are well have no need of a physician, but those who are sick" (Mark 2:17).

Jesus' genuine vision had been at times softened by the evangelists. Jesus' probably genuine "the last will be first and the first will be last" was softened by Mark to "Many who are first will be last, and the last will be first" (Mark 10:31).[14] In this manner Jesus' vision—again, the transformation of everyone and everything by the Kingdom—was revised so as to fit more readily into conventional church wisdom.

Consequently, there is a basis for Rudolf Bultmann's claim that there is a distinction between the Jesus of history and the Christ of faith. The followers who succeeded the Jesus of history and became spokesmen for the new movement altered the vision that Jesus had proclaimed. But they did not alter that vision as Bultmann had claimed, that is, they did not exaggerate the identity of Jesus. Rather they toned down the radical vision of the Presence Jesus had proclaimed.

Their revision took on the moral focus that religion conventionally espoused. They proclaimed that Jesus had revised the value of wealth (Mark 10:17–31) and the value of following the Law (Mark 2:23–28). Jesus may indeed have made those assertions, while the disciples located them as the center of his vision of faith.[15] Bultmann based his reserve about the Christ of faith upon such revisions of the proclamation of Jesus. However, because we enjoy a perspective that Bultmann did not have—a more developed appreciation for the vision that the Jesus of history had expressed—we are able to acknowledge that the evangelists' vision of the Christ of faith was not as radically transforming as the vision proclaimed by the Jesus of history.

Ecclesiastical "Sayings" of Jesus

The Christian community developed and continues to develop statements that defend its claims. Some early church writers, like John the Evangelist, developed sayings of the Jesus of history in such a way that Jesus is envisioned as speaking in defense of church doctrine. That is part of the "high Christology" of John's Gospel; namely John's portrayal of Jesus as fully conscious of his being God and as possessing the wisdom of God. The Jesus Seminar, however, voted to identify only one saying in the whole of the Gospel of John as having originated with Jesus: "A prophet has no honor in the prophet's own country" (John 4:44). All of the other statements in that Gospel were voted to be manufactured by the Fourth Evangelist in support of church doctrine.[16] Another example of a statement attributed to Jesus in support of church doctrine is Mark's prediction that "brother will betray brother to death, and a father his child....But the one who endures to the end will be saved" (Mark 13:12–13). That statement was perhaps used by the Evangelist to interpret the terrible events of the siege of Jerusalem by the Romans in 66–70 CE. [17] Yet it has been imagined to be Jesus' warning for all who survive to the last days.

In summary, those sayings and parables that can be traced back to the oral period of perhaps 30 to 50 CE can possibly have originated with Jesus, though not necessarily.[18] Thus there was great caution during the new quest for the historical Jesus in identifying genuine sayings of Jesus.

The Seminar's Vote on Genuine Sayings of Jesus

The Jesus Seminar voted in agreement that Jesus had articulated some form of prediction of the destruction of the Temple. "Do you see these great buildings? Not one stone will be left here upon another; all will be thrown down" (Mark 13:2). An alternate form of that statement is offered in Mark's trial scene before the high priest: "We heard him say, 'I will destroy this temple [and]...will build another'" (Mark 14:58). E. P. Sanders offered an explanation: Jesus had predicted the imminent appearance of judgment upon the Jewish approach to worship and the consequent emergence of a new age. If Jesus also said, "I will destroy...and will build a new temple," then he presented himself as God's agent in that emergence of the new age.[19] That is, if this saying is genuine, then the Jesus of history indeed presented himself as the Christ of faith, as the one chosen by God to represent the Presence in human history and to inaugurate a form of worship that is more divinely acceptable.

A saying of Jesus that appeared genuine to the third questers is the parable of the evicted demon's finding seven more-powerful friends and with them reoccupying its human host more forcibly. That saying seemed to mirror the reflection by Jesus early in his ministry that his own exorcisms lacked lasting effectiveness.[20] In that saying, Jesus was presenting himself not as the Christ of faith, but as a frustrated prophet with great charismatic gifts. He was conscious that he was acting as the representative of the Presence, even though he appeared to be frustrated by not having the power that most assume to be the characteristic of the Presence.

The parables of the lost sheep and the lost coin (Luke 15:3–6, 8–10) focus, not upon the need of the lost to repent, but upon the fidelity of God in seeking out those who are lost.[21] There was moderate agreement among the participants in the Jesus Seminar that these were genuine sayings of Jesus. If so, then they reveal that Jesus proclaimed, not that sinners (the lost things) need to repent, but rather that they need to trust that God will faithfully seek them out and draw them back. Jesus emerges in his sayings as rarely demanding that sinners seek repentance.

E. P. Sanders went on to insist that Jesus had not proclaimed himself to be the expected son of David, that is, had not envisioned himself as bringing military victories or political autonomy for Israel. Rather, Jesus foresaw the selection of some individuals as saved and others as rejected. The parable of the judgment of the sheep and the goats conveys this understanding. Jesus in that saying did not concern himself with Israel's nationalistic hopes to recover the empire of David.[22] He did not present himself in the form that the people expected the Messiah to have. Instead, he proclaimed a revision of the meaning of the Messiah: the Promised One who summoned individuals to a trusting relationship with God.

Those who heard Jesus summoning them to transform their relationship with the Presence found themselves in a crisis. Many of them had gradually come to recognize that Jesus was far more than a teacher of wisdom, more even than one of the prophets. He had spoken as the Promised One would speak; he had convinced many that he was indeed the Messiah. Those people came to a fork in their lives' paths. They could continue to believe in Yahweh the judge; the Jewish tradition held that Yahweh insisted that believers were to obey the high priests and observe every point of the Law. Or, they could transform their manner of interrelating with the Presence. Jesus told them that the Presence summoned them to live in freedom. If they chose to accept Jesus as the Christ, then they would need to follow *this* directive, but to choose so was to jeopardize their status with the Yahweh for whom the high priests spoke. Such believers faced a severe crisis.

IV   The Actions of Jesus

As in the case of the sayings of Jesus, in the case of his actions, there are genuine actions and imagined actions. The Jesus Seminar in its effort to identify the genuine actions of Jesus used the same four criteria: discontinuity, embarrassment, multiple attestation of sources, and coherence of the occurrences leading to the passion. That last criterion is perhaps applicable only to actions, not sayings. There are actions that identify an individual's fundamental life-choices and lead to the person's taking an irreversible position. In the case of Jesus' actions, an example of a fundamental life-choice is the cleansing of the Temple. When Jesus did that, he drew his line in the sand and challenged the high priests to cross it. They were going to either refuse to cross that line and allow Jesus to claim extraordinary authority, or choose to demonstrate that Jesus possessed no more authority than any other Jew and therefore had to be eliminated.

Jesus in History

Paul, the first New Testament author, wrote his letters approximately one generation after the death of Jesus. Although he had not known the Jesus of history, his identification of Jesus as a historical individual deserves serious consideration.

Paul described Jesus as being born of a woman (Gal 4:4), as belonging to the race of Abraham (Gal 3:16, Rom 9:5), as carrying on the lineage of David (Rom 1:3), as living under the law (Gal 4:4, Rom 15:8), as exercising a ministry to Israel in fulfillment of the promises to the patriarchs (Rom 15:8), and as dying on a cross (multiple references in Paul).[1] One who considers Paul's identification of those actions of

Jesus is challenged to accept Jesus as having been an individual within Jewish history and as having understood himself within the traditions of that history.

Actions of Jesus That Are Securely Affirmed

In the next few generations after Paul's writings, the evangelists agreed—multiple attestation—about the following:

- Jesus was born in about BCE 4, that is, at approximately the time of the death of Herod the Great.
- Jesus was baptized by John the Baptist.
- Jesus was a Galilean itinerant teacher who preached and healed in villages and in town synagogues, but who generally avoided cities.
- Jesus at times effected remarkable cures, including exorcisms, as demonstrations of the truth of his proclamation of the Kingdom of God.
- Jesus spoke Aramaic, Hebrew, and probably some Greek.
- Jesus called disciples and spoke of there being twelve.
- Jesus, with only a few exceptions, confined his activity to Israel.
- Jesus practiced personal prayer in seclusion.
- Jesus summoned people to repent.
- Jesus made use of parables to announce the Kingdom of God.
- Jesus shared in table fellowship with a socially and religiously diverse group, including those whom many Torah-observant Jews would have regarded as sinners.[2]
- Jesus engaged in a controversy about the Temple.
- Jesus impressed his contemporaries as one who spoke and acted with authority, that is, as a charismatic individual who wielded extraordinary power over demons, a power that he then transmitted to his disciples. He also acted as one who bore the authority to forgive sins. In that way he won a degree of popularity.
- Jesus identified his ministry as one of exorcisms, cures, and preaching, when told that Herod Antipas was a threat to him. However, he acknowledged that he would finish soon.

- Jesus made an implicit claim to plenary authority over Israel by his dramatic cleansing of the Temple, that is, he was far more than just another Jewish prophet.
- Jesus ate a final meal with his disciples.
- Jesus was arrested and interrogated by Jewish authorities, apparently by the explicit authority of the high priest.
- Jesus' disciples generally abandoned him after his arrest but "saw" him after his death.
- Jesus was crucified outside Jerusalem by the Roman authorities. The crime written and affixed above his head was "the King of the Jews." This showed that his actions had been understood by the Romans to have been a pretension to royal dominion.[3]
- Jesus died, after which his followers continued as an identifiable movement. At least some Jews persecuted at least parts of that new movement.[4]

Jesus was not only one among many Jews in history, but emerged from his fellows Jews as one who assumed a role of extraordinary importance. As a reflective person, he would have been conscious that he had established an extraordinary difference between himself and his fellow Jews. He did not understand himself to be on a par with those among whom he lived.

Acceptance of John's Baptism

There is a strong tradition by multiple attestation, from not only the four canonical Gospels but all of the eighteen other unendorsed gospels, that Jesus was baptized by John the Baptist. In accepting John's baptism, Jesus was demonstrating his agreement with John's agenda: the restoration of Israel. Matthew's portrayal of Jesus as sending out his disciples on a ministry to Israel provides a confirmation of Jesus' agreement with John's vision. In Matthew's Gospel Jesus charged the Twelve, "Go nowhere among the Gentiles, and enter no town of the Samaritans, but go rather to the lost sheep of the house of Israel. As you go, proclaim the good news, 'The kingdom of heaven has come near'" (Matt 10:5–7).

Moreover, there is no mention of Jesus' visiting the two major Greek cities in Israel—Tiberias and Sepphoris. Seemingly ignoring those two major centers of Greek culture in Israel, Jesus was carrying out the Baptist's vision of focusing, not upon the Greeks, but upon Israel as the domain in which the Presence had returned to reign.[5] Identifying the vision of Jesus with the vision of the Baptist infers that Jesus had been a disciple of John for some time, but then developed his own mission, although still restricting it to those to whom John had preached.

Like John, Jesus preached repentance and baptism in the face of the imminent judgment. He stood as witness to the conversion of the repentant and their ritual sealing in water. His challenge to repent and to change one's attitude toward the imminent judgment was effective: some of John's disciples complained to their master that "here [Jesus] is baptizing, and all are going to him" (John 3:26).[6] Thus Jesus in imitating John's mission had apparently become more effective than the Baptist.

In fact, Jesus expanded his own mission far more than John had intended his mission to be. Jesus, like John, proclaimed the need for repentance at the emergence of the Kingdom. Yet Jesus went on to identify himself as the predicted Messiah. The prophet Third Isaiah had predicted that the Messiah would bring good tidings to the afflicted, bind up the brokenhearted, proclaim liberty to captives, and liberate those who are prison-bound (Isa 61:1, 2). Matthew envisioned John's disciples as bringing a message from John to Jesus asking whether he was the one who is to come. Jesus responded by citing the Messiah's actions in Third Isaiah—just quoted—and thus identified himself as not simply John's former disciple, but the promised Messiah:

> When John heard in prison what the Messiah was doing, he sent word by his disciples and said to him, "Are you he who is to come, or are we to wait for another?" Jesus answered them, "Go and tell John what you hear and see: the blind receive their sight, the lame walk, the lepers are cleansed, the deaf hear, the dead are raised up, and the poor have good news brought to them" (Matt 11:2–5).

Jesus the Prophet

Because of the charism of Jesus' actions, he seems to have been aware of himself as having the authority to challenge his hearers to figure out what his actions meant and to respond to him. He performed extraordinary actions, such as exorcisms and healings, to symbolize that the Kingdom of God is already in the midst of the human community. He apparently performed those actions without explaining them, simply assuming that witnesses would perceive them as symbols of the Presence in their midst. They would also perceive Jesus as the prophet announcing the Kingdom of God. Thus, Jesus seemingly understood himself as much more than a social or moral prophet.[7] On the contrary, he was portrayed as having viewed himself and as having been viewed by others to be the bearer of the prophetic Spirit of the Messiah.

He also promised that same Spirit to others. Thus, during his ministry, he sent the apostles on missions of teaching, healing, and exorcisms, as though they too were prophets.[8]

Consequently, one is challenged to acknowledge that Jesus was aware of himself as bearing the responsibility, not only to speak for, but also to act in place of the Presence and to challenge others to respond to the Presence. He spoke and acted as though the Presence's plan of salvation and justice for both Israel and the world was being unveiled through his own presence, his own work, and his own fate. The evangelists imaged the Jesus of history to have consciously symbolized the unimaginable: the Presence's salvation was occurring in the space-time events of the life of Jesus.[9] He would thus have been consciously, if not frighteningly, aware that he was in some way the Promised One, the Messiah.

Mark portrayed Jesus as having been aware of himself as the Messiah from the beginning of his public ministry. As soon as Jesus had gathered some disciples, he preached in a synagogue in Capernaum. There, a man with an unclean spirit called out that he knew Jesus as "the Holy One of God." Jesus rebuked him and exorcised the unclean spirit from the man (Mark 1:21–28). Mark portrayed Jesus there as someone having authority and power over demons and as having the ability to break their hold over the man with the unclean spirit. That was a new reality and a personal challenge for the audiences of Jesus' time and of later times. Jesus was and is someone who is unique, who represents the Presence, and who was aware of it.[10] Having so presented himself to his followers, the Jesus of history challenged and challenges all to acknowledge his self-awareness of acting in the place of the Presence.

Cleansing of the Temple as Symbolic

Jesus apparently performed an extraordinary action to symbolize the coming destruction of the Temple. That action was in some way also a demonstration that animal sacrifice was no longer an appropriate manner of worshipping, that Temple worship itself was no longer acceptable to the Presence, and that the new and perfect Temple would soon arise.[11] In this action Jesus was vulnerable and selfless in presenting himself, not only as far more than a faithful Jew, but as the one who had received divine authority to preach and to transform worship.

Jesus' interference in the Temple trade (Mark 11:15–19 and parallels)—multiple attestation—may be an action that twenty-first century people find confusing. Yet first-century Jews knew it was a claim to have the authority of the Messiah, to be one who was superior both to the high priests and to the Law.[12]

Symbolic Claims to Be Messiah

The question explored in this book is whether the confession of Jesus as Messiah has anything to do with the historical person of Jesus or whether it is confined to the post-Easter communities of believers. After the resurrection, Jesus was thought by believers to be the Messiah, the Son of God, who had assumed his seat at the right hand of the Presence. However, such a title or designation of a human had been unknown prior to Jesus. Jesus himself must have so acted and spoken as to claim this title. If he had not, then there would have been those among the earliest postresurrection community who had very forcibly resisted the claim that Jesus was the Messiah. Thus, apparently the historical Jesus had felt himself to be standing in a nearness to God such as no one before him had done.[13] Some actions of Jesus—such as the cleansing of the Temple, the exorcisms, and the choice to march into the high priests' trap—must have symbolized to his followers that he understood himself to be identified with the Presence.

The creative imaginations of Mark (Mark 1:9–11) and Luke (Luke 3:21) fashioned other such actions of Jesus symbolic of being the Messiah. Immediately after the baptism of Jesus, a voice from heaven and a hovering dove identified him as the Son of God. Then the Spirit led Jesus into the desert to be tempted to turn away from his vocation of identifying himself and responding as the Chosen One of God.[14] Jesus was portrayed by both Mark and Luke as having chosen to respond positively to the invitation of the Presence and so to identify himself and to act as the Son of God and Messiah.

Luke later portrayed Jesus as having been so completely the Son of God that he participated in the power of the Presence. For example, he commissioned his disciples to have no fear of serpents, scorpions, or enemies and assured his disciples that he would protect them from any harm (Luke 10:19–20). Luke thus presented the historical Jesus as having been aware of himself as someone who dared to act as the Presence would act in human experience.

Mark, Matthew, Luke, and John—multiple attestation—depicted Jesus as having entered into Jerusalem on a colt. This action matched the prophet Zechariah's vision of the Messiah: "Rejoice greatly, O daughter Zion! Shout aloud, O daughter Jerusalem! Lo, your king comes to you; triumphant and victorious is he, humble and riding on a donkey, on a colt, the foal of a donkey" (Zech 9:9). Jesus' having so presented himself to Jerusalem was making a symbolic claim to be the Promised One.

Clearly those who wrote in order to present their visions of the historical Jesus ascribed several of his actions as symbolic of his self-consciousness of being the Messiah.

On the other hand, the evangelists did not portray the historical Jesus as himself using words to claim that he was the Messiah. In the four Gospels, that title is found only on the lips of others, not on his. Nonetheless, it is true that Jesus was not portrayed as having rejected the title.[15] So, the fact that the post-Easter communities acknowledged that Jesus deserved such titles implies that his actions, at least his symbolic actions, had laid claim to them.

Objectivity of Jesus' Walking on Water

The Gospels' descriptions of Jesus' walking on the water—Mark 6:45–52; Matt 14:22–33; John 6:16–21 (multiple attestation)—have all of the hallmarks of reporting an altered state of conscious experience, that is, subjective awareness. The objectivity of such an experience is presented simply as Jesus' subjectivity. Because others, such as we, find that experience to be incredible, it can appear to be socially dysfunctional.[16]

On the other hand, Matthew's story of Jesus' walking on water includes the scene of Peter's entering into the subjective experience of Jesus: Peter joined Jesus in walking on water, even if he walked only briefly. Thus, Matthew's story suggests that Jesus' action of walking on water was not simply Jesus' subjective, altered state of consciousness, but was a socially objective experience. Peter had entered into the event.

As a result, at least Peter, and possibly the other disciples in the boat, experienced the Jesus of history as having a more-than-human power of performing an action that only someone like the Messiah, the Chosen One of the Presence, could have done. They then experienced him in that action as the Christ of faith.

Jesus' Actions to Restore Israel

Since the era of the Babylonian Exile—789 to 728 BCE—Israel had lost its independence as a nation. Jesus' proclamation—the Kingdom of God is in your midst—might have been understood as his decisive intention to restore the Kingdom, though in an altered form. Jesus' proclamation of the Kingdom of God might have signified to the Jews his identifying with the good news of the second author of the Book of Isaiah (chapters 40 to 55). Jesus signaled a new exodus for Israel out of oppression and toward national restoration.[17] There are hints of this understanding in the Gospels. As previously mentioned, Jesus chose not to minister in Sepphoris, the major Greek city in Galilee. This complete bypass might have meant to the Jews that Jesus was concerned exclusively with the restoration of Israel as an independent nation.

One can sympathize with those who interpreted Jesus' actions as suggesting that he at least supported, if not contributed to, the restoration of Israel.

Jesus as "A Wandering Sage"

The Jesus Seminar has identified Jesus as "a wandering sage." While such a designation may be too narrow for Jesus, it does focus upon some of the Gospels' data. Both Matthew (8:20) and Luke (9:58) portrayed Jesus as contrasting himself with the foxes and the birds. The foxes have holes, and the birds of the sky have nests, but the Son of man has nowhere to lay his head—because he wandered from town to town with no fixed home.[18] Indeed, the evangelists did present Jesus as an itinerant preacher.

However, Jesus was much more than a wandering sage. His mission was not simply to preach sermons, nor to offer maxims, nor to gather support. Rather, Jesus' passionate concern was to convince people that Israel's God had actually come as king. They were to pause and to take note that, in the ministry of Jesus and in his actions, the Presence was already among them bringing about the Kingdom of God in an altered form, not the anticipated, conventional form of a nationalist Kingdom of military victory.

Jesus' table-fellowship with sundry individuals, including sinners and outcasts, was his radical proclamation that the Presence was accepting all into the emerging Kingdom.[19] The itinerant preacher Jesus was consumed by his mission of persuading his hearers to rely, no longer upon themselves and their moral righteousness before the Law, but upon the Presence who was gratuitously restoring their relationship with the divine One.

That vision of Jesus was supported by his choice not to focus upon himself. He rarely initiated dialogue, debate, cures, pronouncements, or self-promotion. He made no claim to be the Messiah.[20] Such reserve regarding himself directed his hearers not to himself, but to the Presence who was establishing the Kingdom in their midst.

Jesus as a Symbol of the Radically New

When Jesus was crucified, his crime was fixed above his head on the cross: "King of the Jews." That title would not have been used by his followers, nor by the early Christians, both of whom had identified Jesus, not as the King of the Jews, but as the Messiah or the Son of God.

If, as the Jesus Seminar claims, Jesus had been simply a wandering sage, a pest, or a Cynic—one who asked questions and proposed wisdom—then the authorities would have done no more than imprison and scourge him. Yet they crucified him. His words and actions must have either implied or asserted a royal claim of some sort.[21] He had so presented himself as one who inaugurated an entirely new approach to the Presence. In Israel, a religious state, this was a revolution against not only the Judaism that ruled the state but against the state that was founded upon the stability of the Jewish religion. Such a revolution would easily have been interpreted by the Jewish and Roman authorities as a royal claim by Jesus.

Jesus had cast out demons as one who has authority even over Satan and who is more powerful than Satan. Such a radically new authority had seemingly frightened many of his audience. Mark's Gospel stated that some identified Jesus as receiving his authority from Beelzebub, the prince of demons (Mark 3:22). Mark then portrayed Jesus as having responded with the parable of the binding of the strong man (Mark 3:27). Mark's Jesus thus acknowledged that he operated outside of the conventions, that he acted with a power to bind Satan such as no other had, and that he indeed had extraordinary authority. He assumed the right to operate outside of official Jewish channels; demons obeyed him. One can well understand why some of his audience would have claimed that he acted with the power of the prince of demons.[22] In any case, Jesus certainly acted in such a way that his audience and the Roman authorities could not but assume that he was inaugurating a radically new order with a previously unknown power.

Luke mirrors Mark in the portrait of Jesus as having broken away from the sacred convention of religious customs. John had "come eating no bread and drinking no wine" and had been interpreted to have so broken from custom that he had a demon. Conversely, Jesus had come eating and drinking and had been interpreted to have so broken from custom that he was a glutton and a drunkard, a friend of tax collectors and sinners (Luke 7:33–34). Yet both John and Jesus symbolized in their actions that there was occurring an eschatological change: the Presence who had always been present in history was, in the Baptist's and Jesus' surprising actions, more fully present and active. Jesus' table-fellowship with sinners was not acquiescence to their moral status; rather, he symbolized the gratuity of the universal reign of God. Some of those who shared table with Jesus, like Zacchaeus the tax collector, responded to that invitation to participate in the Kingdom with a moral conversion (Luke 19:1–10).

Jesus' parable of the prodigal son appealed to the righteous, symbolized by the elder brother, to imitate the eschatological response of the father by reconciling with sinners. Otherwise, the righteous would be contradicting the universal gratuity of the reign of God.[23] Because Jesus was proclaiming the radically new universal presence of the reign of God in history, he symbolized a profound break with social conventions: table-fellowship with all, even with those who were outside the Law.

Another act of Jesus that trumpeted the in-breaking of an entirely new era was his driving out the "Legion" of unclean spirits from the possessed man in the country of the Gerasenes. The location of that story—Gerasene, on the eastern shore of the Sea of Galilee and thus outside of Galilee or Judea—is decisive evidence that the event was historical. Later Christians would have had no reason for locating Jesus there. The response of the people who witnessed that exorcism—they asked Jesus to depart from their region: the criterion of embarrassment—indicates that they recognized that Jesus was inaugurating a new era (Mark 5:1–20). They preferred not to acknowledge that such a revolution was beginning. In driving Jesus away, they hoped not to have to confront such an era of novel power.[24] People who fit in well with the accepted religious conventions apparently were not willing to risk becoming vulnerable to this eschatological and revolutionary era.

Perhaps the most radical act of Jesus was his criticism of Temple worship and of the power of the high priests, that is, generally, the Sadducees, in Jerusalem. His cleansing of the Temple (Mark 11:15–18; Matt 21:12–13; Luke 19:45–48; John 2:13–17) confronted the Jews with the challenge of an entirely transformed era. Jesus demanded that the worship of the Presence be no longer a Jewish concern; that the high priests were no longer to be allowed to regulate worship.[25] While some responded positively to this challenge, others rejected Jesus as a royal pretender.

Jesus Acted Eschatologically

Both Ben F. Meyer and N. T. Wright [26] identified the Jesus of history as having proclaimed the eschatology of the messianic hopes of

Israel: the end-time of restoration having already arrived in the ministry of Jesus. Yet the messianic hopes of Israel remained unfulfilled, that is, not yet fully present. The traditional era of Jewish worship was ending and was to give way to the new worship centered upon the access to the Presence that Jesus promised and symbolized in his actions, such as the cleansing of the Temple.

Jesus had begun his ministry in relation to John the Baptist. The Baptist had been an eschatological prophet who called Israel—already-present believers—to repent in view of the coming Kingdom, the domain that would include the not-yet-present Gentile believers.

Paul the apostle was later to reverse that vision of the Baptist. Paul had envisioned that the Gentiles would be the first to be already-present believers in the Kingdom of God; then as a result of Paul's Gentile mission, Israel would be the not-as-yet-present believers in the Kingdom.[27] From the start of Jesus' ministry, according to Paul's vision, he had represented to his audience the eschatology of the Presence's working salvation.

That not-yet-fully-present fulfillment of Israel's messianic hopes, as Paul envisioned it, was symbolized by Jesus in his Temple action. His cleansing of the Temple, and claiming that the Temple would be destroyed and rebuilt, invited his audience to recall Isaiah 49:5–6: the Lord would restore "Jacob," that is, the tribes of Jacob, through the Suffering Servant. Then salvation would reach to the ends of the earth, that is, to the Gentile world. Jesus' cleansing of the Temple, and pledging that a spiritual temple would replace the material Temple, exemplified his vision of salvation reaching far beyond the borders of Israel, even to the end of the earth.[28] Jesus' audience would have been conscious that, in risking to suffer by attacking Temple worship, Jesus was identifying with the prophet Deutero-Isaiah's Suffering Servant who was engaged in achieving universal salvation through his own suffering.

The Temple action of Jesus—the cleansing of the Temple—is overwhelmingly defended as a historical event. Not only does it have multiple attestation, but the trial-scene accusation that Jesus threatened the Temple embarrassed the early church. Apparently, the church had to acknowledge that Jesus had physically and verbally attacked the sacred center of Judaism and thus deserved condemnation (Matt 27:39). The same embarrassing acknowledgment is found in Stephen's speech (Acts 6:13): Stephen's accusers charged that he, like Jesus before him, had attacked the

Temple. They said, "For we have heard him say that this Jesus the Nazorean will destroy this place and will change the customs that Moses handed on to us." Jesus had done something extraordinary in the Temple and said something about its destruction. Whatever Jesus did, it must have been resented by the Temple hierarchy, that is, by those who had a vested interest in the profit derived from the sale of bird offerings and the exchange of money. Those were the high priests of the Sadducees, who had combined religion with the politics and economics of the Temple. Jesus' action did not effectively terminate money changing. However he acted—perhaps he overturned a few tables—he symbolized the destruction of the Temple, the end of Temple worship, and the subsequent establishment of a new form of divine worship.[29] In a dramatic symbol, Jesus broadcasted that the new era, the Kingdom of God, was already present, even if it was not yet fully present. The former era of Temple worship was at an end. The eschatological age had dawned.

The temptation of Jesus by Satan in the desert is another eschatological action that is supported by multiple attestation (Mark 1:12–13; Matt 4:1–11; Luke 4:1–13). The evangelists' texts portrayed Jesus as going into the wilderness and besting the temptation to give up proclaiming the eschatological Kingdom of God. He lived by faithfully acting as the Spirit led him, although he had to confront either his own misgivings or an external resistance that argued about the folly of such action.[30] Even if Jesus could not demonstrate the certitude of the Kingdom as already present, he acted to convince many that the Kingdom was both already present and soon to be more present.

A new manner of proceeding was introduced by Jesus' actions. That manner was portrayed by John the Evangelist in his image of Jesus washing the feet of his disciples at the Farewell Meal (John 13:2–11). Washing someone's feet in first-century Palestine was a task that only a servant or a slave would be expected to do. John's Gospel portrayed Jesus as conscious of already being uniquely "Lord," yet deliberately acting like a slave for others, and summoning his followers to do likewise. Jesus' summons is found elsewhere in the New Testament. Mark 10:43–54 presents Jesus as having taught that "whoever wishes to be first…must be slave of all. For the Son of Man came not to be served, but to give his life as a ransom for many." The hymn in Philippians 2:5–11 similarly focuses upon Christ who "did not regard equality with God something to be exploited, but emptied himself, taking the form of a slave." Jesus' action of washing the feet of his disciples was understood to be a symbol that the Kingdom of God is already present.

Apparently Tertullian and Origen cite the practice of foot-washing among first-century Christians as an action that was a sign of their belief in the eschatological Kingdom.[31] Jesus' dramatically symbolic action greatly encouraged his believers to participate in his belief in the Kingdom as eschatologically present.

The actions of the Jesus of history expressed his personal self-understanding as the Christ of faith, as the one who acted and acts for the Presence and who summoned and summons all to follow him in interrelating with the Presence.

V   Jesus, Miracles, and Crowds

The historical data regarding Jesus as the Christ certainly includes the extraordinary signs that the evangelists portrayed Jesus as having performed. Three of the evangelists, Matthew, Mark, and Luke, identify those extraordinary actions as "miracles." The Evangelist John identifies them as "signs" that the Kingdom of God is breaking into human history. Those signs or miracles appear to have been genuine: three criteria for authenticity (embarrassment, coherence, and multiple attestation) indicate their authenticity.

The Jesus who performed those signs was acknowledged by Matthew as having extraordinary authority: "When the crowds saw [Jesus' cure of a paralytic], they were filled with awe, and they glorified God, who had given such authority to human beings" (Matt 9:8). Eventually, the crowds responded to Jesus as being not only a miracle-worker, but as the Promised One, the Messiah, the expected new David, the one who was to be their king, even the one who represented the Presence to them. Jesus was unique to his people in that he was a miracle-worker, a moral teacher, a gatherer of disciples and followers, and an eschatological prophet—all those in one person.[1] In short, the crowds identified him as the Christ.

Miracle-Worker or Magician?

There has been a debate regarding whether Jesus worked miracles or magic. Some have compared Jesus with Apollonius of Tyana. Apollonius, who died in about 98 CE, was a Neopythagorean philosopher, a virtuous man, and a religious teacher. Long after his death some anti-Christian writers composed biographies of him in order to portray him as the equal of Jesus. Those biographies have been used in modern time to disparage the uniqueness of Jesus by drawing alleged parallels between Apollonius and him.[2]

Those who witnessed the miracles of Jesus learned from him that the miracles pointed not to Jesus, but to the presence of the Kingdom of God among humans. As a result, the crowds confessed Jesus as the herald of the Presence, then as the Christ of God.

Multiple Attestation of Jesus as Miracle-Worker

Those who are interested in the historical basis for the miracles of Jesus will want to give special attention to the multiple attestation of sources to those miracles. Every gospel source—Mark, Q, Matthew, Luke, and John—along with the Jewish historian Josephus, affirms the miracle-working activity of Jesus.[3] One would be closed-minded to go against such an accumulation of affirmations of the historical Jesus as a miracle-worker.

For example, even the Q tradition, which is made up almost entirely of sayings, nonetheless contains one miracle story, the healing of the centurion's servant (Matt 8:5–13 and parallels). This suggests that the editor of the Q sayings realized that Q needed to include at least one miracle story if its image of Jesus was to be accurate.

Next, there are in the Synoptic Gospels various sayings that testify to general knowledge of Jesus as a miracle-worker. For example, there is a dispute in Matthew 12:22–32 about whether Jesus performed exorcisms by the power of Beelzebub or by the "finger of God."[4] The question was not whether Jesus performed the miracles, but which power gave him the authority. His having performed great signs was too widely accepted to deny.

Then Josephus, also known as Joseph ben Matthias, provided non-Christian and very early evidence of Jesus as a miracle-worker. Josephus wrote two great works: *The Jewish War* and the much longer *Jewish Antiquities* (circa 93–94 CE). In that latter book Josephus, who had no religious reason to proclaim Jesus, wrote, "At this time [the rule of Pontius Pilate as prefect of Judea] there appeared Jesus, a wise man....He was a doer of startling deeds, a teacher of people who receive the truth with pleasure. And he gained a following both among many

Jews and among many of Gentile origin."[5] Such non-Christian and secular evidence of Jesus as a "doer of startling deeds," as a miracle-worker, is indeed arresting.

The evangelists even portrayed Jesus as having raised the dead: the daughter of Jairus (Mark 5:21–43), Lazarus (John 11:1–46), and the son of the widow of Nain (Luke 7:11–17). Three distinct evangelists agreed that their portrait of Jesus' public ministry should include the proclamation that Jesus had even raised the dead,[6] thereby heralding that Jesus had acted as no mere human could act.

Jesus' Charism for Attracting Crowds

The public miracles by Jesus emerged from the gospel portrayals as responses to peoples' faith and as invitations to believe. Apparently great numbers of people surrendered themselves not only to Jesus' invitation to believe, but also to repentance—the acknowledgment that the Kingdom of God was in their midst—and to discipleship. The evangelists portrayed the wonder-working Jesus as having attracted interpersonal relationships with the crowds who had witnessed his wonders.[7]

In fact, the indictment against Jesus as "King of the Jews" was brought against him by the Sadducees, not only because they thought that Jesus claimed to be king, but also because they thought that the crowds had appeared to want him to become their Messiah-king.

One cannot but wonder, therefore, why Mark the Evangelist often referred to the Twelve's failure to believe. The Sadducees had perceived that many in Jesus' audience had too much faith in him. So why did Mark portray the Twelve as having the contrary response? Perhaps he was developing the theme that, while multitudes choose to entrust themselves in belief, there are always some of the selected ones who do not choose to trust the Other.

Doubt regarding the wondrous "signs" of Jesus is apparent. However, the second criterion of the Jesus Seminar, coherence, is met: the miracles of Jesus converge, mesh, and support his other actions and sayings. All flow into the same proclamation that the Presence dwells in and acts with power within the human community. That was the focal theme of Jesus' ministry.[8] If Jesus did such signs and offered such evidence of the Presence among humans, then one has even more difficulty in comprehending Mark's indictment of the unbelief of the Twelve and such people as the Gerasenes.

Not only the chosen rejected the charism of Jesus the wonder-worker. The exorcism of the Gerasene demoniac (in Q and in Mark 5:1–20) is a unique miracle in several ways. One is that the Gerasenes rejected Jesus after he had performed the wonder before them. They asked Jesus to leave their district.[9] There may have been other crowds who refused to trust in Jesus, even as he worked great wonders before them.

Jesus' Feeding the Crowd

All four canonical Gospels recount the miracle of Jesus' feeding the crowd: Mark 8:1–10; Matthew 15:32–39; Luke 9:10–17; and John 6:1–15. Mark included two versions of the story. An exegete is able to discern in those accounts the traces of the evangelists' representation of Elisha's feeding of the starving crowd (2 Kgs 4:42–44). Nonetheless, the multiple attestation suggests that the story of Jesus' having fed the crowd reaches back to the earliest days of the first Christian generation.

Jesus' feeding of the crowd also supports his proclamation that his hearers would experience the Kingdom of God as a banquet—the principle of coherence.

The exegete may conclude that Jesus had at least once fed a large crowd with only a few fish and some bread.[10] Such an action in front of the large crowd would have been strong sensual evidence that Jesus acted as no mere human could have acted. Rather, he presented himself to the crowd as one who, for them, represented and acted for the Presence as the expected Christ was to act.

Jesus' Other Nature Miracles

Nature miracles, like the feeding of the crowd, are those that involved Jesus' changing natural elements.

The miracle of changing water into wine at the wedding feast of Cana is found only in the Gospel of John (John 2:1–11). The exegete, therefore, may well consider it to be less than certain as a historical event.

On the other hand, the walking on the water is found in three Gospels: Mark 6:45–52; Matt 14:22–33; John 6:16–21 (multiple attestation). The story had apparently been part of the Jesus tradition in the first Christian generation and is continuous with the early church's confession of Jesus as divine. It presents the theme of Jesus as revealing himself as acting with a power that appeared to be divine. Jesus acted as being the promised Messiah, the Christ of the Presence. Thus in Matthew's story, the apostles who witnessed the walking on water responded in a choral profession of faith in Jesus: "Truly you are the Son of God" (Matt 14:33). Yet, despite multiple attestation, the criterion of discontinuity fails to support the genuine history of the walking on water. Psalm 77:20 envisions the Messiah as walking on water. Nonetheless, multiple attestation does lead the reflective individual to be slow to discount the walking on water as a genuinely historical event.

Jesus' calming the storm at sea (Matt 8:23–27; Mark 4:35–41; Luke 8:22–25) is the story of a nature miracle that appears in each of the Synoptic Gospels but not in the Johannine material. Multiple attestation, then, does not completely support the event as genuinely historical. So, too, Jesus' cursing the fig tree (Mark 11:12–14, 20–21; and Matt 21:18–20) is a story of a nature miracle that appears in only two gospel sources. One would expect that such a startling action would have been retained in the other two gospel sources as well.[11]

One who reflects upon the stories of Jesus' nature miracles may conclude that Jesus indeed had fed the crowd and walked on the water. Even though one has less solid data in support of the other nature miracles, one must acknowledge the evidence that suggests that Jesus had power to change some elements of nature. He thus acted in front of others as only one with divine power could act. Those who witnessed such nature miracles saw Jesus present himself as the divinely chosen Christ. Before there was a church to fashion and proclaim that Jesus is the Christ, there were crowds who had witnessed his mighty deeds and therefore had proclaimed him to be the Christ whom the Jews had expected.

VI Jesus' Interpretation of the Law Presenting Him as the Christ

Jesus summoned an unidentified disciple with the words, "Let the dead bury their own dead" (Luke 9:60). The demand to leave the dead to bury their dead is unlike anything known in Judaism or in early Christianity. By the criterion of dissimilarity then, that expression is probably a genuine saying of Jesus.

The basic thrust of that expression is that the law of being a disciple of Jesus overrides all other laws, traditions, and responsibilities, whether oral or written. Jesus consciously asked for disobedience of the burial commandment, which was understood to be binding upon all Jews because of a tradition received by divine revelation.[1] Jesus summoned (and summons) his followers to proceed along the path of fidelity to himself, rather than to the Law, laws, or traditions.

Foundation for Jesus' Power to Reinterpret Law

One may well ask by what right Jesus chose to reinterpret laws that had been believed to be divinely inspired. The evangelists frequently had Jesus use the expression "Amen, I say to you" to indicate his self-awareness of having prophetic-charismatic authority. He apparently perceived himself to know directly and without scribal study what the Presence willed in any given situation. Jesus needed to reinterpret the Law if he was to be faithful to the Presence, who personally revealed the divine will to him. Consequently, Jesus reinterpreted the meaning of working on the Sabbath (Mark 3:1–6 and parallels); the extent of the community that one is to love (Matt 5:44 and parallels);[2] and the range of possibility for divorce (Matt 19:3–9 and parallels).[3] Those who claim to accept and to trust Jesus are challenged to accept as well his radical reinterpretation of the will of the Presence; in other words, to acknowledge that will as the Presence reveals self in each situation, rather than as any written form of law or tradition that claims to convey the will of the Presence.

Reinterpretation of the Law as Revolution

In reinterpreting the Law, Jesus called into question its adequacy. The Law need not be applied in a given situation. Those who choose to follow Jesus on that path of openness to the Spirit were, and are, exposing themselves to being vulnerable before those who assume that *they* have the certitude of written law. The ground upon which disciples stand in following Jesus into revolution is that they share with Jesus his hope that in the new age there will be a better order; that the new age will in some ways duplicate the original creation.[4] They do not follow Jesus because of demonstrable certitude or provable achievement.

Jesus as Sovereign over the Law

Apparently, Jesus saw himself as sovereign over the Law and as the power who decided which parts of the Law needed to be obeyed or not. For example, he saw himself as the power that could restrict the Mosaic tolerance for divorce and expand the range of Sabbath observance and of Sabbath dietary laws.

That revolutionary position of Jesus was seemingly too radical for some of the earliest followers of the Way. For example, there were believers in Galatia who had insisted that Jewish Sabbath laws be kept, that being followers of Jesus did not exempt believers from external observances (Gal 4:10).[5] Such reserve before the challenge to become, necessarily, revolutionaries is certainly understandable in any community that needs to maintain civic order.

Criterion of Multiple Attestation

There is strong evidence that Jesus presented himself as empowered to reinterpret the Law. Not only all of the gospel sources, but also Paul and Deutero-Paul (the author of 2 Thessalonians, Colossians, and Ephesians) show Jesus as having reinterpreted the Law so that it was adjusted to the human context. The meaning of Sabbath obligations, for example, emerged for Jesus from specific human situations (Mark 2:21–28; Matt 12:1–12; Luke 6:1–9; John 5:9–18). Paul and Deutero-Paul portrayed Jesus as having insisted that the meaning, not only of the Sabbath obligations, but of the entire Law needed to be reinterpreted as the Spirit suggests, within the human context (Rom 2:12–27; Gal 5:3–23; Eph 2:15).

Response to Jesus as Reinterpreting the Law

In order to approach the influence that Jesus would have had in so reinterpreting the Law, one needs to recall the social and religious context of first-century Judaism in Israel. In that context the interpretation of the Law was in the hands of the Sadducees. They claimed to have the exclusive right to interpret the meaning of the Law in every situation. Without any apparent compassion for those who bore the burden of obedience, they required of all Jews civil compliance with the Law. Consequently, the Jews in the first century found the Law to be a significant hardship, even an oppression.

From that perspective, one may gain a sense of the impact upon first-century Jews that Jesus would have had in his insistence that the Law was to be reinterpreted within the human context, as the Spirit indicates. The burden and oppression of the Law evaporated readily. Thus, many of the Jews enthusiastically responded to Jesus; his teaching on the humanity of the Law transformed religion into a humanizing endeavor.

Therefore, many began to identify Jesus as the Messiah-king and to urge that he assume the position that convention thought would be the position of the Messiah-king, namely, the new David, the King of the Jews. Jesus' mission of interpreting the Law as human led many

Jews to identity him as that Messiah, the Christ. What is more, they moved to elevate him as Christ to a position of power.

That popular enthusiasm for Jesus as deserving to be king was probably one of the most powerful forces that led the chief priests to judge that they needed to eliminate him. They had no tolerance for any uneducated peasant's claims that rendered the chief priests to be irrelevant in interpreting Jewish observance. There may well have been a swell of enthusiasm for Jesus as being the Messiah-Christ. Nonetheless, the chief priests would not have been able to join in that enthusiasm; they could not believe that the Christ would possibly oppose the traditional powers of Judaism.

VII Jesus' Consciousness of Being Messiah

To uncover the consciousness of self of someone in ancient times is a challenge that appears incapable to do. Nonetheless, the Jesus Seminar has proposed that its criteria for genuine historical occurrences in the life of Jesus (embarrassment, multiple attestation, discontinuity, and coherence) can direct those interested in uncovering Jesus' self-consciousness. There are indeed New Testament statements about Jesus' being conscious of his elevated status as Messiah. If one or other of those satisfies one or other of the above criteria, then it can be judged that Jesus probably did understand himself to be somehow the promised Messiah.

Gospel Vision of Jesus' Claim to Be the Messiah Promised in the Old Testament

The evangelists formulated their vision of Jesus not only by committing to writing the community's memories of how he had explicitly presented himself to his audiences; they also portrayed Jesus as having been conscious of his fulfilling Old Testament passages regarding the Messiah and as having, therefore, claimed to be the one who was promised.

Matthew's Jesus responded to the Pharisees' question about his relationship with the Messiah by citing Psalm 110:1: "The Lord says to my lord, 'Sit at my right hand until I make your enemies your footstool.'" That psalm promised that the Messiah would share Yahweh's throne, would sit at the right hand of the Presence. Matthew's Jesus had thus consciously claimed to be the Messiah.

Moreover, both Matthew and Luke had identified Jesus with "the stone that the builders rejected" in Psalm 118:21–24. They used the psalmist's vision of the rejection of the Savior-Messiah as their own. Both Matthew and Luke identified Jesus with the stone, interpreting the Jewish and Roman authorities' rejection of him as the fulfillment of the vision of the Messiah in Psalm 118.

Luke in Acts portrayed Jesus as having envisioned himself as the one whom the psalms had promised as the Messiah. In Acts 2:25, Luke quoted Psalm 16:8 to identify Jesus with the Davidic Messiah. Peter's speech in Jerusalem on the day of Pentecost used that passage from the Hebrew Scriptures to persuade the assembled crowd to place their trust in Jesus: "I saw the Lord always before me, for he is at my right hand so that I will not be shaken." That assembled audience of Jews would have known that the following three verses of the quoted Psalm 16 are a prayer of trust that the Lord will remain always faithful to the Messiah.

In Acts of the Apostles 2:30–31, Luke went on to have Peter's speech quote Psalm 132 and immediately after that, Psalm 16: "Since he was a prophet, he knew that God had sworn with an oath to him that he would put one of his descendants on his throne. Foreseeing this, David spoke of the resurrection of the Messiah, saying, 'He was not abandoned to Hades, nor did his flesh experience corruption.'" In Acts of the Apostles 4:25–26, Luke had Peter in the same speech quote Psalm 2:1–2: "[I]t is you who said by the Holy Spirit through our ancestor David, your servant, 'Why did the Gentiles rage, and the peoples imagine vain things? The kings of the earth took their stand, and the rulers have gathered together, against the Lord and against his Messiah.'" In those passages, Luke recalled that the Hebrew Scriptures expected the Messiah not simply to be a victor, but to be one who would suffer rejection, endure shameful death, and need to rely upon the mercy of the Presence.

In Matthew's Gospel, messengers from John the Baptist came to Jesus to ask whether he was "the one who is to come," that is, the Christ. Matthew envisioned Jesus to have responded with First Isaiah's vision of the identity of the Messiah: "[T]he blind receive their sight, the lame walk, the lepers are cleansed, the deaf hear, the dead are raised, and the poor have good news brought to them" (Isa 29:18, 26:19, and 35:5–6). In Matthew 11:5, Jesus laid claim to being the Messiah promised by First Isaiah. There Jesus had been pointing to the activities of the Presence who had sent him to act as Messiah in place of the Presence among the people of Israel.[1] One might well note that Jesus was remembered there as having been conscious of being the Messiah.

The Romans' Indictment of Jesus as a Messianic Pretender

The Romans' indictment of Jesus as deserving death was fastened to the cross above his head: "Jesus of Nazareth, King of the Jews." There were those who had perceived Jesus to have claimed and acted as a royal or messianic pretender.

In the Markan trial scene (Mark 14:53—15:20), there are motifs of Jesus' claiming to be Messiah: his claim to destroy the Temple and to replace it with self (Mark 14:58); also his claim to be the Messiah, the Son of the Blessed One, seated at the right hand of the Power (Mark 14:61–62). Those Markan motifs provide an intelligible ground for the Jewish accusation that Jesus had blasphemed and thus deserved death.[2] His claim that he would build the new Temple in three days was interpreted by the Jews as a claim by Jesus that he possessed a mysterious, unfathomably transcendent and, therefore, divine authority.[3] Such a claim would certainly have driven the Jews to accuse him of blasphemy, of a conscious claim to be the Chosen One through whom the Presence acted among the Jews.

The criterion of embarrassment confirms the claim by Jesus that he was greater than the Temple. If Jesus in that environment had claimed to supersede the Temple, then he would have been guilty before the Law of consciously pretending to have claimed to be the royal Messiah-king.

The criterion of multiple attestation also suggests that Jesus during the trial scene had genuinely claimed to be the Messiah. Not only Mark (14:53–65), but also Matthew (26:63–64), Luke (23:2–3), and (John 18:33–37) portrayed Jesus in the trial scene as having claimed to be the Christ, the Messiah, the Promised One who had come from God to Israel.

Mark's Gospel presented Jesus from the perspective of "low Christology," that is, perceived as a charismatic human who proclaimed the Kingdom of God and who presented evidence that he spoke with authority that far surpassed human power. Mark did not interpret Jesus from the perspective of "high Christology," from the perspective of Jesus as a divine man. Thus, Mark's portrayal of Jesus on trial as having claimed to be the Messiah, the Son of the Blessed One, is discontinuous with Mark's general interpretation of Jesus. This criterion of discontinuity suggests that those claims by Mark's Jesus were genuine, that Jesus had indeed been conscious of being far more than Mark generally identified Jesus to be, and that Jesus had been conscious of being both the Messiah and the Son of God.

The leaders of the Jews apparently took those conscious claims by Jesus to the Roman authorities and revised them so that they were claims that Jesus had appeared to have been a royal pretender to replace Caesar.

Jesus' Redefining the Meaning of "Messiah"

During the hearing of Jesus before Caiaphas in Mark's passion narrative, Caiaphas asked Jesus whether he was the Messiah. Jesus answered, "I am; and 'you will see the Son of Man seated at the right hand of the Power,' and 'coming with the clouds of heaven'" (Mark 14:62). Mark envisioned Jesus as claiming to be the Messiah foreseen by the prophet Daniel (Dan 7:13)—the one like a Son of Man coming on the clouds of heaven, who received dominion and glory and royalty. The significance of Jesus' response is immense. While a prisoner in danger of being executed, Jesus identified himself as the Messiah foretold by Daniel, thereby redefining the meaning of "the Messiah" as not the new David, not a military and a political victor, but as one who is vulnerable and who suffers.

On the other hand, Jesus identified the meaning of the Messiah as apocalyptic or as beyond the grasp of human imagination. Mark's portrayal of Jesus' response to Caiaphas used the words of the apocalyptic book of Daniel (Dan 7:13) and implicitly referred to the apocalyptic vision of Daniel 7:12: "As for the other beasts, their dominion was taken from them, but their lives were prolonged for a season and a time"—Daniel's effort to form images of the Messiah's incomprehensible victory. Mark's reference to that apocalyptic image identified Jesus as having been conscious of being the unimagined Messiah, but of being the Messiah in an apocalyptic, that is, unimaginable, manner.

Matthew's portrayal of Jesus also presented him as redefining the meaning of the Messiah. As Matthew envisioned Jesus' reflection on the failure by the people of Jerusalem to respond to him, Matthew portrayed him as having presented a radical vision of himself as Messiah: "How often have I desired to gather your children [the people of Jerusalem] together as a hen gathers her brood under her wings, and you were not willing" (Matt 23:37). This picture that Jesus posed suggested a hen in a barnyard fire, when her chicks are in danger. The hen gathers her chicks under her wings. Jesus had envisioned by his reference that, when the fire has run its course, there would be found a dead hen scorched and blackened, but under her wings the live chicks. Jesus had thus proposed that, by his messianic self-sacrifice, he would turn the divine wrath away from Israel.[4] The conventional meaning of Messiah had been the new David, the new military and political power, who would use his own force to reunite Israel and to reestablish Jewish autonomy. Yet Jesus, in his image of a mother hen in a barnyard fire, had consciously redefined the meaning of Messiah to be a self-sacrificing victim of death for the sake of those who are dependent on him.

Physician and theologian Albert Schweitzer recognized that Jesus had redefined the meaning of the Messiah by acknowledging that Jesus had deliberately gone up to Jerusalem, where he knew that the Jewish high priests had laid a trap for him. Thus, he expected and intended to suffer execution there. Schweitzer saw in Jesus' expectation and intention that he had yet in another manner consciously redefined the meaning of the Messiah to be apocalyptic and eschatological. Definitely this Messiah was unimaginable in relation to the conventional expectations of the Messiah as a military and political power. Recall that eschatology is the tension between the already present (messiah) and the not-yet-fully present (messiah). By choosing to walk into the trap, Jesus was pointing to his persecution and death as the achievement of the not-yet-fully-present Messiah.[5] How radically different Jesus had defined the meaning of the Messiah. Jesus envisioned the Messiah to be a victim, who was vulnerable to the political powers that rejected him.

Jesus' Consciousness of Being Messiah

Jesus acted and taught in such a manner that he seems to have been acutely conscious that he was acting as the representative of the Presence to Israel. His actions and teaching made sense only if Jesus was aware that the Presence was even then, in his words and deeds, present and active in the new manner that had long been promised. Moreover, his proclamation that he would build a new Temple, not built with human hands, indicated his consciousness that he was the prophet, the Messiah, the one who was making the long-absent Presence return to be among the people. The new community of Yahweh would be the new community that consisted precisely of Jesus and his people.[6] Whether or not contemporary New Testament scholars are able to determine to their own satisfaction that Jesus said he was the Messiah, such speech and actions by Jesus indicate that he obviously was conscious of being the Promised One.

Furthermore, Jesus was conscious of himself as far more than a wandering sage, as the Jesus Seminar has identified him. He had a strong sense of his unique value as a prophet to the people of Israel. That is evident in his having taken the initiative in issuing peremptory commands to follow him—commands that brooked no opposition or delay. He demanded that those whom he called were to physically accompany him on his preaching tours and thus to leave behind their homes, parents, and livelihoods, even as they followed Jesus without geographical or temporal limit; he demanded them not just to risk their day-to-day living, but also to be willing to accept hostility and suffering, even at the hands of their families. Jesus' demands to his disciples were so radical and absolute that his command to follow him was something far different from following him as the crowd followed him.[7] To have gathered disciples indicated that Jesus was conscious of having the power to initiate an extraordinary new movement. His commands and teachings were evidence that he was aware of initiating the kind of new movement that had been promised long ago and had been earnestly sought by the Jewish people.

Perhaps most revealing of Jesus' awareness of being far more than a wandering sage and even the Messiah was his intense proclamation that the reign of the Presence had been dawning with his ministry. Furthermore, Jesus proclaimed that the Presence was among the people gratuitously, not as the consequence of their legal or moral uprightness. Moreover, the Presence was not only among the Jews but among the nations and there renewing the world, as Second Isaiah's "Servant Songs" had envisioned the achievements of the Messiah.

Jesus prophesized that every hearer was to accept the offered salvation in simplicity and with the gratitude that a child shows for a gift. Obviously Jesus had been aware of his work as being the work of the eschatological Messiah.[8] Conscious of acting and proclaiming the Kingdom, Jesus was evidently aware that he acted with an extraordinary mandate from the Presence. He was revising the meaning of how the believer was to interrelate with the Presence. He was challenging the people of Israel to turn from their fidelity to their legal observances and, rather, to follow in every experience the Spirit of the Presence whom they came to recognize in the ministry of Jesus.

Matthew portrayed Jesus as having preached in the Sermon on the Mount "Do not think that I have come to abolish the law or the prophets; I have come not to abolish but to fulfill" (Matt 5:17). The Jesus Seminar voted to identify that statement as probably a genuine saying of Jesus. Moreover, in that declaration Jesus claimed to be bringing the words of the prophets to fulfillment.[9] Evidently Jesus was conscious of himself as competent to satisfy the expectations and hopes that the prophets had inspired in the people of Israel, the hopes that they had placed in the Promised One.

Jesus' Forgiveness of Sins as Messiah

All the evangelists (multiple attestation) portrayed Jesus as having forgiven sins, even the sins of those who lived outside the Law. He welcomed all kinds of sinners, even tax-collectors, to his table-fellowship. He offered words of forgiveness and largess to those who were considered living outside the Law and, therefore, who did not conform to the Jewish image of those deserving the good favor of the Presence. Jesus assured such people that their faith granted to them what only the Presence could give them, namely, forgiveness of sins.[10] In acting so, Jesus was certainly conscious that he was capable of acting and speaking as no one else, other than a speaker for the Presence, could act and speak.

Jesus, the "New Temple"

The image of Jesus as the new Temple synthesizes many of his actions, sayings, and proclamations. Jesus implicitly claimed to be the place where and the means by which Israel's God was at last personally present to and with the people. Jesus took the immense risk of acting as if he personally were the Shekinah—the Presence's dwelling among the people—as if he personally were the presence of YHWH tabernacling with them. In other words, Jesus was the incarnation of the living Presence for Judaism (Matt 5:17–20).

Some of Jesus' parables (one example is the parable of the sower —Mark 4:26–29) manifest his claim that by his ministry he was the Temple. He functioned for Israel *as* the Temple, which was for them the ground upon which seed is scattered; the earth within which the Presence's scattered seed produces the harvest. He functioned for them as the manifestation of the word of the Presence to them.[11] In fashioning such images of himself, even if those images were implicit, Jesus presented himself to his audiences as the Messiah.

The Temple for first-century Judaism was the place where the living God was believed to be present and to be *experienced* as present with the people. Jesus perceived himself to be called by the Presence to be for the people what they had understood the Temple to be, namely, the place where the Presence encounters them. Jesus upstaged the Temple, took on its role and function, and legitimatized those actions with the claim that he acted for the living God.[12] He challenged his Jewish audiences to accept him as one who was far more than any mere mortal could be.

The Messiah in the Temple

The most obvious evidence that Jesus launched a messianic claim for himself was his symbolic action of judgment in the Temple—the cleansing of the Temple. The high priests challenged him to give them a sign of his authority for disrupting the exchange of moneys in the Temple. In response Jesus answered them, "Destroy this temple, and in three days I will raise it up" (John 2:19 and parallels: multiple attestation).[13] With those words he laid claim to the kind of eschatological power that no one other than the Messiah could claim.

The Risen One's Self-Awareness

The resurrection awoke the dejected disciples to the truth that Jesus continues to be the Messiah. From this they concluded both that he was indeed the Lord of the world, as the Messiah was always supposed to be, and that his death, rather than being a shameful defeat, was in fact the strange, but glorious victory over all forces of evil. From that combination of beliefs, they went forward to declare that Jesus was somehow to be identified as the personal manifestation, the embodiment of the one God of Israel.[14] That was the impact of the resurrection upon the disciples of Jesus. Imagine what its impact had been upon Jesus himself. One can surmise that he had first formulated the beliefs in himself as Messiah, which the disciples repeated. Then, when the Presence had raised him from the dead, Jesus must have become acutely conscious that he *was* the personal choice by the Presence as the promised Messiah.

VIII Jesus' Symbols of His Consciousness of Being the Christ

The Christian community of believers has fashioned symbols of Christ that may appear to be quite different from the symbols that the gospel narratives fashioned for him. In the first generation after the death of Jesus, the community produced the symbol of Christ as he who "will come again." Then in the mid-twentieth century, Teilhard de Chardin, a paleontologist, created an evolutionary reinterpretation and symbol for Christ: "the Alpha and the Omega."[1]

The Gospels presented "Christ-symbols" that Jesus, who understood himself to be the Christ, had fashioned for himself. Searching for the causes of the Jews' drive to execute Jesus, one must confront Jesus' attacks, both implicit and explicit, upon the standard symbols of the Jewish worldview during the second-Temple era (516 BCE–70 CE). He had turned away from those conventional Jewish symbols, not because he judged that they were wrong or evil, but because they had become out-of-date and belonged to the period before the coming of the Kingdom of God. In their place, he presented symbols of his own ministry in order to redefine the meaning of Israel.[2] One needs to remain sensitive to how the people of Israel, especially the high priests, whose religious symbols were presumed to make the Presence active among the Jews, would have reacted to Jesus' symbols.

Symbol of "The Twelve"

In order to articulate clearly his concern for the whole restored Israel, Jesus chose an inner circle of disciples, "the twelve." The Twelve had long been the symbol for the twelve tribes of Israel that played a historic role in establishing the first communities of Jews. Jesus used that symbol as the number of his closest disciples in order to proclaim that his mission was to all of Israel. He taught that, in his own mission, the Presence was coming in power to gather and rule all Israel.[3] How startling, therefore, it is to discover that, although the Gospels presented Jesus as concerned almost exclusively with a mission to the people of Israel, soon after his death those closest disciples, the Twelve, initiated a mission to the people of the whole world. The probable motive for that widened mission was the Risen One's revelations to the Twelve that they were to broaden the horizons within which they were to minister. Nonetheless, one cannot help but be surprised at the contrast between the nationalist concern of Jesus and the internationalist concern of the early communities after he had risen.

Gratuitous Forgiveness

Jesus represents the symbol of gratuitous forgiveness for all. He did not place any expected condition upon forgiveness, such as the forgiven person then becoming faithful in Temple-worship or Temple-sacrifice. He did not even require that sinners definitely commit themselves not to sin again. Rather, on his own authority, he offered gratuitous forgiveness to all, being the contemporary equivalent of a private individual who offers to personally issue to someone a passport or a driver's license, and thus circumventing the law. Jesus thus was undercutting the official system and assuming the right to establish his own system in its place.[4] In his mission to Israel he presumed to have the authority that derived only from the Presence—only the Presence could forgive sin. Jesus thus consciously acted as only the chosen representative of the Presence could act.

All Welcome in the Kingdom

Jesus also gratuitously healed any who drew from him a response of compassion. He did not limit his healing to those who were faithful in their practice of Judaism nor did he restrict his healing only to Jews.

Furthermore, Jesus inverted the meaning that was then conventionally given to suffering. In the first century, and often in the twenty-first century, suffering was and is considered as a curse by God upon those who had or have been unfaithful. Jesus challenged that symbol of suffering as divine punishment. His healing of Jew or non-Jew alike was his new symbol of suffering as a summons of divine compassion.[5] Jesus was so aware of his representing the Presence to Israel that he judged himself empowered to modify religious symbols. He changed the meaning of suffering as a symbol and even initiated new such symbols by introducing suffering as a symbol that summons divine compassion.

Symbols of Jesus' Royal Messianic Claim

Jesus performed two powerful symbolic actions as he came to Jerusalem for his last Passover: he approached Jerusalem in a triumphal entry, and he cleansed the Temple. He did these in order to make present his claim to be the royal Messiah who reigns over David's ancient capital and over the Temple originally built by David's son Solomon.

Those two powerful symbolic actions help explain why Jesus was arrested and tried on that particular visit to Jerusalem and why Pilate condemned him to death on the charge of claiming to be the King of the Jews.[6]

In so acting, Jesus certainly appears to have consciously claimed to be the promised Messiah, the son of David, the one sent to Israel by the Presence, even somehow the expected successor to David the king.

Symbol of the Farewell Meal

In the first century, the Jews considered the Temple to be the greatest Jewish symbol. Yet on the evening before he was arrested, Jesus proposed his own alternative religious symbol, the Kingdom-feast. All the values in the Temple-symbol were integrated and resynthesized in Jesus' Farewell-Meal symbol.[7] What kind of an individual was Jesus, who fashioned a symbol to be repeated in remembrance, not of the Yahweh of the Hebrew tradition, but of himself? Jesus would have created a replacement symbol for the Temple only if he was conscious that he represented for Israel all that the Jewish people hoped to receive from the Presence.

The earliest interpretation of the Farewell Meal is found in Paul's 1 Corinthians: "For I received from the Lord what I also delivered to you, that the Lord Jesus on the night when he was betrayed took a loaf of bread…and said, 'This is my body that is for you.…[And taking the cup, he said] This cup is the new covenant in my blood.…Do this…in remembrance of me'" (1 Cor 11:23–25). One may appropriately note that Paul there cited Jesus as the origin of that interpretation. Jesus apparently revealed to Paul that he, Jesus, had interpreted the Farewell Meal as a symbolic action that binds its participants in covenant-communion with him and that he had intended it to symbolize his death as expiation for all and as a covenant sacrifice.[8] This may startle those who have assumed that the early community, not Jesus, had fashioned the symbols of the sacred elements as representing Jesus and of the crucifixion as a covenant sacrifice. Indeed, the First Letter to the Corinthians, which is the earliest New Testament text, recognized that Jesus was the source of those interpretations. As early as 55 CE, when Paul wrote that letter, Jesus had revealed himself to Paul as the Savior Christ who is symbolically present in the Eucharist and whose death saved all.

Symbol of the Kingdom of God

Jesus apparently led his followers to trust that the Kingdom of God was "coming to be" in his mission; that the Kingdom was present in his words and deeds. He offered no hint that the Kingdom would come on condition that humans would achieve it, certainly not that moral righteousness or the force of arms that brought about David's kingdom would bring the Kingdom of God to be present. On the contrary, Jesus offered the symbol of the Kingdom as representing an eschatological kingdom. The Kingdom "is like a mustard seed" (Matt 13:31), which is already planted, is already here, and appears to be the least important of seeds—not yet the great shrub that it will one day become.[9] As Jesus envisioned the power of the Presence, the greatness of the Kingdom will simply emerge by the work of the Presence. It will not depend upon any kind of human achievement, whether military, political, or moral.

Zeal of Faith, Not of Observance of the Law

In proclaiming that the Kingdom of God is here, Jesus changed the religious symbol of zeal from being a passion to observe the Law to a passion to trust that the Presence is working in every event of history. In so changing the referent of their zeal, the audiences of Jesus would indeed become the light of the world, the salt of the earth, the liberation of those who in any way endorse religious values.

In his supreme freedom regarding the observance of the Sabbath laws (Mark 2:24–28), Jesus summoned his audiences to trust, not in religious conventions, but in his person and his relationship with the Presence, who alone is bringing about the eschatological Kingdom.

In his challenge to his hearers that they revise the Jewish dietary code, Jesus called forth from them a free attitude toward diet in light of their trust in the gratuitous working of the Presence in their midst. In his challenge to the claim of descent from Abraham as a birthright entitling one to unshared privileges, he indicated that many peoples are chosen by the Presence. In his driving out the money-changers from the Temple, he acknowledged that religious symbols are not absolute, but relative to the conditions for prayer.[10] Such liberating actions and words were a summons to assume zeal in trusting the Presence, who was active in the ministry of Jesus and who remains active within the human community. Jesus obviously was aware of offering to Israel a radically new approach to divine worship.

IX Early Devotions and Expressions of Faith

During his life Jesus had symbolized himself as the Christ. As centuries followed one another, the early Christian communities fashioned further symbols of Jesus as the Christ. Individuals today can identify such symbols that have been influential in their own life.

The earliest expressions of faith by the earliest Christian communities have been termed *Proto-Orthodox Christianity*. These communities were not monolithic in belief, as they are often mistakenly said to be, but instead were comprised of an interesting variety of expressions and practices. From about 70 to 170 CE, Proto-Orthodox Christianity maintained, on the one hand, a high regard for the traditions of the Hebrew Scriptures and for Jewish monotheism (belief in the one God), as well as a critical suspicion of radical innovations to that tradition. On the other hand, Proto-Orthodox Christianity manifested a readiness to accommodate a certain critical diversity of faith.[1] In the earliest Christian communities were Jews who strove to be faithful to their Jewish roots, but also Christians who deliberately expanded their Jewish faith to include faith in Jesus of Nazareth as the promised Messiah.

The beliefs of Proto-Orthodox Christianity reveal to those in the twenty-first century the earliest identifiable confessions of faith in Jesus as Christ.

Jesus Confessed as Present in the Eucharist

As the previous chapter noted, as early as 55 CE (the date of the writing of Paul's First Letter to the Corinthians, only one generation after the death of Jesus), the Christian community practiced devotion to Jesus as the one who was present to them in the eucharistic celebration:

> For I received from the Lord what I also delivered to you, that the Lord Jesus on the night when he was betrayed took a loaf of bread, and when he had given thanks, he broke it and said, "This is my body that is for you. Do this in remembrance of me." In the same way he took the cup also, after supper, saying, "This cup is the new covenant in my blood. Do this, as often as you drink it, in remembrance of me." (1 Cor 11:23–25)

Not only did those first Christians recognize very early the Jesus of history as Lord, but they also trusted in his received words to have symbolized his continuing presence to them as the Christ who with his followers had celebrated the Farewell Meal as the Jesus of history.

Jesus Confessed as the Savior and Redeemer

Just two generations after the death of the Jesus of history, the Christian community firmly identified the Jesus of history, not only as the Christ of faith, but also as Christ the Savior, the one who has saved us from our sins; as Christ the Reconciler, the one who has reconciled us with the Presence; and as Christ the Redeemer, the one who has redeemed us. Evidence reveals that the Christ whom the community preached and worshipped was for them identical with the Jesus of history.

Jesus Confessed as Second to the Presence

A few generations later, Justin Martyr in his *First Apology* stated that the Christian community of the early second century practiced devotion to Jesus "as Son of the true God Himself, and holding Him in the second place" (*First Apology* 13), thus confessing Jesus as second only to God. Those very early Christians worshipped Jesus both as the Christ and as God, not simply as the charismatic Jesus of history.

Since Justin Martyr lived between about 100 and 165 CE, his testimony, too, is very early—just five generations after the death of Jesus.[2] This along with Paul's 1 Corinthians challenges those who argue, as Rudolf Bultmann argued, that the Christ of faith is distinct from the Jesus of history. Paul's and Justin Martyr's writings regarding Christian belief lay before us evidence that the very early Christian community acknowledged the Jesus of history had become for them the Christ, the promised Messiah, the one who stands second only to the Presence, no less than the Son of God.

X Jesus and the Gentiles

Although Sepphoris was the major city in Galilee during the life of Jesus, the New Testament makes no mention of this Greek-speaking city. Similarly, Caesarea, also a Greek-speaking city, was the major city in Samaria. Again there is no gospel story that locates Jesus in Caesarea of Samaria. The assumption is that, because Jesus restricted his ministry to Jews, he did not journey to any Greek populations.

On the other hand, there are gospel stories about Jesus' ministry to the Gentiles.

There are two versions of the banquet parable (Matt 22:1–10 and Luke 14:16–24). The king held a wedding feast for his son, yet the invited guests would not come. The king then sent his servants to "the roads and lanes" (Luke 14:23) to compel people to come in. There is no restrictive adjective attached to "people." The implication for those who interpret that parable is that the Lord sent out servants to both Jews and Gentiles.

Another gospel story about Jesus' ministry to Gentiles is his curing the paralyzed servant of the Roman [Gentile] centurion. The Roman centurion responded with the faith that acknowledged Jesus to have authority similar to his own:

> The centurion answered, "Lord, I am not worthy to have you come under my roof; only speak the word, and my servant will be healed. For I also am a man under authority, with soldiers under me; and I say to one, 'Go,' and he goes; and to another, 'Come,' and he comes; and to my slave, 'Do this,' and he does it." (Matt 8:8–9)

In the story Jesus then praised the faith of the centurion:

> When Jesus heard him, he was amazed and said to those who followed him, "Truly I tell you, in no one in Israel have I found such faith. I tell you, many will come from east and west, and will eat with Abraham and Isaac and Jacob in the kingdom of heaven, while the heirs of the kingdom will be thrown into the outer darkness, where there will be weeping and gnashing of teeth." (Matt 8:10–12)

In Jesus' foretelling that "many will come from east and west and eat with Abraham and Isaac and Jacob in the kingdom of heaven," he suggested to those who seek to interpret his meaning that the many who will come and sit with the patriarchs are like the centurion, non-Jews. Thus, the story indicates that Jesus intended to eventually expand his ministry to include the Gentiles.

Still, his general mission as recorded in the New Testament was to the people of Israel. Sending his disciples out on a mission, he said, "Do not go into pagan territory or enter a Samaritan town. Go rather to the lost sheep of the house of Israel." Before they set out, he forewarned them, "you will be dragged before governors and kings because of me, as a testimony to them and the Gentiles" (Matt 10:5–18). In that and the parallel passage, Mark 13:10, the New Testament envisions Jesus as having expanded his ministry to the Gentiles, even as he sent his disciples out to the Jews. Governors and kings are rulers in Gentile lands where they will bear "testimony before them and the Gentiles" as well as to the people of Israel.

Nonetheless, one cannot simply ignore the New Testament restriction of the ministry of Jesus to the Jewish people: "I was sent only to the lost sheep of the house of Israel" (Matt 15:24) was Jesus' response to the Canaanite [Gentile] woman who asked him to exorcise the demon who possessed her daughter. Even though Jesus did eventually exorcise that daughter, the story certainly portrayed him as reluctant to extend his ministry beyond the people of Israel.

Paul acknowledged that the early Christian community in Galatia in Asia Minor was open to the expansion of Christian ministry to the Gentiles. There was some disagreement among the Christians regarding the terms and the conditions of that ministry, for example, whether the

Gentiles needed to observe Jewish dietary laws and circumcision (Gal 2:7–14). However, there was no objection by the Jewish Christians in Galatia to Paul's carrying the good news to the Gentiles. Some interpret the early community's openness to embracing Gentile converts as evidence that Jesus himself had preached that the community of believers was gradually to include Gentile believers, that the Presence was as willing to welcome the Greeks as the Jews. Perhaps Jesus had deliberately not withheld the disciples from expanding their ministry to include Gentiles.[1]

So, although there is evidence that Jesus generally, but not always, restricted his ministry to the Jewish people, there is also evidence that, in the first generation after Jesus' death, his disciples had understood him to have approved of their expanding their ministry to include the Gentiles.

"Christ" to the Gentiles

The assumption of Rudolf Bultmann and of many others is that the meaning of the Christ of faith was fashioned and preached by the community of Gentile believers, and that the meaning of the Jesus of history is quite distinct from that meaning of the Christ. However, the evidence cited here suggests that the Jesus of history had himself extended his ministry to the Gentiles.

Jesus would therefore have been aware that he would become for the Gentiles a beacon of hope in the darkness. He would have been conscious that the Gentiles would find him to be the one who would transform the meaning of life for them and become for them the Christ whom they would proclaim. He would have known that he was for them the unexpected source of healing (the cure of the possessed daughter of the Canaanite woman), as well as the hope for those who sought spiritual security in the material world (those from east and west who come to eat with the patriarchs in the Kingdom of Heaven).

Thus, the Jesus of history apparently intended that his followers would present him to the Gentile world as the Christ in whom they would trust, in whom they would find hope, and because of whom they would expect to live forever in the Kingdom of God.

The Jesus of history had directed his mission to eventually embrace the Gentile world and had chosen to become that Christ whom the Gentiles would fashion.

XI The Indictment Brought Against Jesus

The criteria that the Jesus Seminar used in their research concerning Jesus as a criminal before Roman justice are again embarrassment, multiple attestation, discontinuity, and coherence. Those will be beneficial in an effort to identify the crimes or causes that led to the indictment against Jesus.

Theologies of the Crucifixion

One might well acknowledge that, from the earliest days after the death of Jesus, there have been attempts to explain it not as the result of a crime that he had committed, but because of the theological meaning of it. Thus Paul's 1 Corinthians 15:3–5, Mark 14:21, and other New Testament references insisted that Jesus was crucified "according to the scriptures." Apparently that reference to the scriptures was recognition that Jesus' death had been described in Psalm 22:16–18:

> For dogs are all around me;
>   a company of evildoers encircle me.
> My hands and feet have shriveled;
> I can count all my bones.
> They stare and gloat over me;
> they divide my garments among themselves,
>   and for my clothing they cast lots.

or Psalm 41:8–9:

> They think that a deadly thing
>   has fastened on me,
>   that I will not rise again from where I lie.
> Even my bosom friend in whom I trusted,
>   who ate of my bread, has
>   lifted the heel against me.[1]

Seemingly, there are some believers who remain satisfied with the citation of those texts; they believe that Jesus suffered crucifixion so that the Hebrew Scriptures—that is, at least those two psalms—might have found in his execution their promised fulfillment.

Others explain the crucifixion as the consequence of Jesus' having followed out his messianic vocation. Again, the Hebrew Scriptures (for example, Second Isaiah's five songs of the Suffering Servant) envisioned the Messiah as empowered to ransom the world and those who had died, empowered to give life to the world, if he quietly and trustingly suffered his own execution. Mark the Evangelist went so far as to identify the divine mission of Jesus: "For the Son of Man came not to be served but to serve, and to give his life as a ransom for many" (Mark 10:45). Some use such scriptural citations as evidence that Jesus understood his prophetic vocation to include the challenge that he suffer a violent death for others. They envision Jesus, when he was on the brink of death, as having offered his death as expiation for the world, "for many" (Mark 14:24), "for the forgiveness of sins" (Matt 26:28), "for you" (Luke 22:20), or "for the life of the world" (John 6:51). Some of those who so explain the death of Jesus are content to rely upon those scriptural claims as the adequate and complete explanation for why Jesus was executed.

Indeed, perhaps as Jesus loved others and increasingly handed himself over for them (Gal 2:20), as he loved his own to the end (John 13:1), as he freed others from sin because he loved them (Rev 1:5), he gradually realized that his choice to be vulnerable for the sake of others was leading him to suffer a horrible execution.

The Indicted Jesus as the Christ

The value of those theological explanations of the indictment against Jesus is that they portray the Jesus of history as the Christ. They represent, however, the vision of Jesus as the Christ because the community of believers after the death of Jesus had decided to portray him that way. At least that was Rudolf Bultmann's thesis, namely, that Jesus as the Christ is the interpretation that the church formulated after he had died.

Indictments Because of Actions by Jesus

There are others who insist that, if the Romans had judged that Jesus deserved death by crucifixion, then Jesus had committed some crime deserving of death. However, then one must search in the scant historical data to find out what that crime might have been.

Jesus' Crime in Forgiving and in Interpreting the Law

As stated earlier, in forgiving sins, Jesus effectively assumed the right to put himself in the place of and to act in the place of the Presence. As the scribes said in Mark's Gospel, "Why does this fellow speak in this way? It is blasphemy! Who can forgive sins but God alone?" (Mark 2:7).[2] If one imagines oneself to be a first-century Jew who had known that only the Presence could forgive sins, yet who had heard Jesus telling another Jew that his or her sins were forgiven, then one can imagine the horror, the scandal, to Jewish faith that Jesus had caused when he forgave sins.

Similarly, Jesus must have caused scandal when he confronted the Pharisees regarding their legalist and externalist view of religious observations. Jesus opposed their self-righteous conviction that their fidelity to external Jewish law won for them merit or good favor with the Presence. He envisioned, rather, that the Presence grants the divine self in a gratuitous manner to all, even to sinners who live "outside the Law."[3] Yet first-century Jews accepted the convention that the Pharisees were

competent to interpret how and why Jews were to observe the Law—the
Presence asked Jews to serve Yahweh by faithfully observing the Law.
One may well recall that Jesus apparently had no acknowledged training
in the interpretation of the Law. Thus, when the Jews heard Jesus not
only reinterpret the Law, but also reject the Pharisees' conventional interpretation, then some, perhaps many, of them would have been horrified
at his assuming a position above that of the Pharisees.

Moreover, Jesus had been convincing more and more of the Jews
in Galilee and Judea that he, not the Pharisees, was the one in whom
they were to place their trust. He had been developing into a demagogue or at least a seeming demagogue: he appeared to have been
using popular religious prejudice among the people to gain personal
power for himself.

When the Romans had assumed power over Israel, they granted
to the chief priests the power to govern and to lead the Jewish people
in their exercise of religion. The chief priests would, therefore, have
regarded Jesus and his accumulation of power with immense resent-
ment and distrust, feelings that developed into a passion to eliminate
him. He threatened their own position. In addition, he threatened the
civil order of the religious state of Israel.[4] The chief priests perceived
Jesus as endangering the delicate balance of power between the Jewish
authorities and the Roman occupiers. They would have needed to
eliminate that threat.

Furthermore, Jesus accused some Pharisees of hypocrisy and
offended some of them by assuring sinners that the Presence was with
them. When the Pharisees manifested horror at such gratuitous forgiveness of sinners, Jesus then accused the Pharisees of being legalistic and
externalist in their bigotry. That accusation is presented in the parable
of the Pharisee and the tax collector (Luke 18:9–14). While the Pharisee
in that parable presented himself to Yahweh as self-righteously upright
because of his fidelity to legal obligations, the tax collector presented
himself as in need of the compassion of the Presence. So while the
Pharisees claimed that they spoke in the place of God, Jesus claimed
that he had the right to speak for the Presence and that the God of
Abraham and Moses had become dissatisfied with claims to moral self-
righteousness. Moreover, Jesus had been growing more and more suc-
cessful in persuading the crowds to acknowledge his claim.[5] The
Pharisees, the Jews' official legal interpreters of the Law, would therefore

have needed to eliminate Jesus as the serious threat to their right to interpret.

The criterion of embarrassment can be cited here. The early church frequently described Jesus as challenging the religious authority of the Pharisees. That citation portrayed Jesus as a religious scandal, an embarrassment to the young Christian community that was asking its members to accept the authority of its leaders.

Jesus' Crime Against the Temple

All of the gospel sources (criterion of multiple attestation) portray Jesus as having so acted as to insult the Temple (criterion of embarrassment) and thus as having attacked not only the high priests, but most Jews, even those who were only marginally observant. All Jews regarded the Temple with pride and joy as the symbol of the Presence within their midst.[6] The official religious leaders of the Jews would not have allowed anyone who had attacked the Temple to have continued to move about freely.

Moreover, Jesus claimed that sinners would be in the Kingdom of God. He did not even demand that they had to turn away from sin before they would be in the Kingdom. Thus those who faithfully worshipped in the Temple and worshipped the Presence by observing the Law would have been insulted by Jesus' apparent disregard for the value of Temple-worship in his granting to sinners entrance into the Kingdom of God.[7] If the authorities of Judaism intended that Judaism was to continue to be a religion of the Temple, then they would have needed to eliminate the demagogue who was successfully persuading faithful Jews that the value of the Temple was passé.

To some extent, perhaps to a great extent, Jesus had committed those crimes. He would so have acted within the religious state of Israel only if he had understood himself to have been the Chosen One, the Promised One, the Messiah, the Christ. Otherwise, he would have accepted the conventional Jewish leaders' directives regarding the practice of Judaism.

The Enemies of Jesus

The Pharisees as such largely disappeared from the last chapters of the Gospels (the curtain came down on them in Mark 12:13, Matt 22:15, Luke 19:39, and John 18:3). However, the scribes and the chief priests, especially the high priests, assumed the prime role as enemies of Jesus in all the Synoptic Gospels (Mark 12:12, Matt 21:45, and Luke 20:19). The chief priests were constantly portrayed as the principal Jewish leaders committed to eliminating Jesus.

The secular ruler, the Roman procurator, held the primary power. Under him the chief priests and the high priests held their power. They were enabled by the Roman procurator to rule by imposing laws according to their own views with or without the approval of the Pharisees. Those priests exercised a strict superintendence[8] of the Law regarding the pursuits of everyday life: diet, Sabbath behavior, home architecture, litigation, and the punishment of condemned persons.[9] So one who seeks to identify those who brought charges against Jesus—and who worked together with the Roman procurator to condemn him—must acknowledge the chief priests as the principal enemies of Jesus, those who indicted, prosecuted, and condemned him.

The chief priests apparently indicted Jesus because he claimed to be "King of the Jews," or at least appeared to claim to be a king in his liberating his audiences from the need to obey the chief priests' interpretation of worship of the Presence. In claiming the right to forgive sins, to welcome those outside the Law to enter the Kingdom of God, and to attack the Temple, he was acting as King of the Jews. Then, in entering Jerusalem while riding on an ass (Matt 21:2–3), he symbolically acted as the king who was foretold by Third Isaiah (Isa 62:11): "Say to daughter Zion, 'See your salvation comes; his reward is with him, and his recompense before him'" and by Zechariah (Zech 9:9): "Lo, your king comes to you, triumphant and victorious is he, humble and riding on a donkey, on a colt, the foal of a donkey." Moreover, Jesus' disciples and an increasingly larger number of Jews in Judea expected him to have a role in the reestablishing of the kingdom of David. Thus, the chief priests needed to eliminate him as a direct threat to their power.[10] To an extent the Gospels portrayed Jesus as just such a threat. In claiming to be the king and apparently the promised

Messiah, Jesus had become vulnerable to the chief priests' anger spawned by their need to maintain their power over the Jews.

The Effort to Humiliate Jesus

After the death of Jesus, the chief priests apparently persuaded the Roman procurator to have Jesus buried in shame. He was buried "where no one had ever been laid" (Luke 23:53), that is, not in a Jewish burial ground where a respected Jewish body would have been buried. The chief priests had a custom of insisting that the bodies of those guilty of crimes were undeserving of decent burials among the honored dead. So they would not have permitted Jesus to be buried as an honorable Jew. The Roman procurator supposedly allowed Joseph of Arimathea to bury Jesus in a place apart from honored dead Jews, thereby conceding to the chief priests their insistence that Jesus was to be buried in shame.[11] The chief priests had been thus most committed to treating even the dead body of Jesus as worthy of no respect. Jesus must indeed have greatly offended them by his presenting himself as one who in their opinion had erroneously claimed to be someone of extraordinary importance.

XII The Resurrection of Jesus

One might well imagine the disposition of the disciples of Jesus after the crucifixion. Jesus would have then seemed to them to be a discredited prophet who had been crucified like a number of other Galilean upstarts who had their hours and then vanished into the shade of public execution. Luke recorded a glimpse of that disposition of the disciples in the Emmaus story: "We had hoped..." (Luke 24:21).

Why then did the New Testament proclamation of Jesus identify him as now reigning as Lord, as overcoming his own death and the deaths of all others, as continuing his ministry amidst his followers?

The disciples uniquely experienced Jesus after the crucifixion; they described that experience as the resurrection. Because of that experience, they proclaimed, not their initial desolation at the crucifixion, but their confident trust that Jesus is the glorified Lord and that his whole career had been eschatologically directed to future universal salvation.

Indeed, something amazing occurred after Jesus died.[1] Consequently, in the initial moment in the history of the community of Christian believers, there was solid trust that Jesus was not only the Promised One, but was the unique one who had conquered death, the one who had saved all humans. Jesus encountered a select number of individuals after he had died.

The Earliest Confession of Jesus as "Christ"

Paul's writing of the First Letter to the Corinthians is recognized as having emerged from the Jerusalem community in the year 39 CE, less than a decade after Jesus died. It reads:

For I handed on to you as of first importance what I in turn had received: that Christ died for our sins in accordance with the scriptures, that he was buried, and that he was raised on the third day in accordance with the scriptures, and that he appeared to Cephas, then to the twelve. After that, he appeared to more than five hundred brothers at once, most of whom are still living, though some have fallen asleep. After that he appeared to James, then to all the apostles. Last of all, as to one born abnormally, he appeared to me. (1 Cor 15:3–8)

Thus, within a decade of Jesus' death, the common faith of the Christian community of the Middle East used the quoted formula that identified Jesus who had died and who then encountered some people as "Christ." Those earliest believers had learned from their initial experiences of the Risen One that "Christ died for our sins," in other words, that he had died because of a divine plan to free all humans from guilt and to assure them of salvation.[2] That passage from the First Letter to the Corinthians predates the composition of any of the Gospels. It documents the community as having recognized Jesus as being the Christ from the very earliest recorded moments in which the Risen One began to form the community of Christian believers.

In those nascent days of the community, there was certainly a consciousness of Jesus as crucified; he had died as a rebel king. He had not liberated Israel from its oppressors, the Romans, and had apparently not even attempted such a liberation. On the contrary, the Romans had conquered him by executing him. Jesus had not rebuilt the Temple. However, he had, as he promised, replaced it. In response, the first members of the community of believers insisted that he was the Messiah who had transformed the world and their worldview, their symbols, their behavior, and their interpretation of Jesus: Jesus Christ is the conquering Lord who continues to act victoriously in history even after his death.[3] Most evidently, after Jesus had died, he so convincingly encountered his disciples that they confessed him not only as their executed leader, but as their victorious Christ.

The Risen Body of Jesus

In his encounters with his disciples after his death, Jesus had not appeared to them as a resuscitated corpse. In the gospel proclamations of almost every appearance of the Risen One, there were portrayals of some of the witnesses as not having recognized that he was Jesus, as not having believed, or as having doubted. Obviously the risen body of the Christ was not simply the resuscitated body of Jesus. It was indeed in some ways a physical body, that is, not a nonmaterial angel or a spirit. Yet it was also transphysical in the sense that it could come and go through locked doors. The body had been transformed from a corpse to a new mode of being physical.[4] Because those whom the Risen One encountered experienced him as transformed by death into a victor over death, they confessed him thereafter as the Christ.

Paul's Confession of the Risen One's Encounter with Him

About midway through the first century, Paul wrote about his personal experience of the Risen One's having encountered him. One needs to recall that Paul had not known Jesus, had despised the movement that Jesus had started, and had most likely judged that Jesus was most properly confined forever to the shades of Hades. Yet one generation after the death of Jesus, about 48 CE, in the Letter to the Galatians (chapters 1 and 2), Paul confessed that God had raised Jesus from the dead. Then in 54 CE, in the First Letter to the Corinthians (especially 3:10–15) and between the years 56 and 59 CE in the Letter to the Romans (especially in chapter eight), Paul confessed that the creator God had fulfilled the ancient promises to Israel, by not only raising Jesus from death, but also thereby saving the people from their sins. Moreover, Paul confessed that he himself, a nonbeliever, had received a personal revelation of the Risen One and had experienced the risen body of Christ to be, not a resuscitated dead body of Jesus, but a living body that is the prototype for the resurrection of all God's people at the end of days. Paul experienced the Risen One as the hope of all for the future.[5] The Risen One was for Paul, in the first generation after the death of Jesus, the promised Messiah.

In Paul's Letter to the Philippians, he adapted a pre-Pauline hymn (Phil 2:5–11) to celebrate the universal lordship of Christ:

Let the same mind be in you that was in Christ Jesus,
who, though he was in the form of God,
    did not regard equality with God
    as something to be exploited,
but emptied himself,
    taking the form of a slave,
    being born in human likeness.
And being found in human form,
    he humbled himself
    and became obedient to the point of death—
    even death on a cross.
Therefore God also highly exalted him
    and gave him the name
    that is above every name,
so that at the name of Jesus
    every knee should bend,
    in heaven and on earth and under the earth,
and every tongue should confess
    that Jesus Christ is Lord,
    to the glory of God the Father.

This hymn contemplates the depth of Christ's humiliation in being crucified and the height of his exaltation in being raised from the dead. It confesses Jesus as the preexistent divine one (2:6) who received from God the identity "that Jesus Christ is Lord, to the glory of God the Father" (2:11). Thus, all people of Israel could confess the Risen One as Lord and Christ.[6] Already in 55 CE, when Paul wrote the letter, the community who used that hymn was confessing Jesus as Christ, not simply as the itinerant preacher from Nazareth.

XIII   The Gospel of Thomas

The apocryphal Gospel of Thomas was written in about 60 CE, prior
to the Gospels of Mark, Matthew, Luke, and John. It is approximately
contemporaneous with Q, with John's source, the book of signs and
with Paul's letters. The Gospel contains one hundred and fourteen sayings (including parables) ascribed to Jesus. It contains no account of
Jesus' birth or childhood (and thus should not be confused with the
second-century Infancy Gospel of Thomas, which is sometimes titled
without the first word). It also contains no account of Jesus' public
ministry, trial, death, or resurrection.[1] The Gospel of Thomas is valued
by several New Testament scholars as providing some genuine sayings
of Jesus, in addition to sayings not found in any other of the sources
for such sayings.

Thomas's Confession of Christ

Even this earliest Gospel confessed Jesus to be of divine origin.
Saying 18 summons the elect to see their own true immortal nature,
which they have learned of by the revelation of the one who came from
the Presence:

> The disciples said to Jesus, "Tell us, how will our end
> come?" Jesus said, "Have you found the beginning, then,
> that you are looking for the end? You see, the end will be
> where the beginning is. Congratulations to the one who
> stands at the beginning: that one will know the end and will
> not taste death." (Thomas 18:1–3)

The elect are thereby to become divine like Jesus:

> Jesus said, "Where there are three deities, they are divine. Where there are two or one, I am with that one." (Thomas 30:1–2)

The book did not identify Jesus as a redeemer; there is no suggestion in the book that humans are sinners in need of redemption. Nor did the book in any way imply that Jesus made his sacrifice to the Presence for the sake of others. Nonetheless, it did present Jesus as being divine and as summoning the elect to become similarly divine.[2]

The effort to discern whether the earliest community was aware of Jesus as divine or whether it created the divinity of Jesus cannot dismiss the Gospel of Thomas. It presents persuasive evidence.

In addition, the Gospel of Thomas offered no indication that the divinity of Jesus posed for its audience a problem that required defense, excuse, or even a pause in confessing belief. Rather, it indicated that the humanity of Jesus, that is, the bodily existence of Jesus, was much more difficult for its readers to accommodate.[3] Those who confessed Jesus as divine would likely have found his bodily limitations (his need for sleep, his growing tired, his fear in Gethsemane) to be arguments against his divine status. Such believers might have become Docetists, those who confessed Jesus to be divine, but only to appear to be human.

Jesus the Revealer, the Exemplar

The author of the Gospel of Thomas presented Jesus as the teacher who revealed crucial insight into the true nature of things. Jesus taught the origin and the destiny of the elect as well the model by which they were to live. Jesus in this Gospel came from above and entered the world to bring illumination to the elect so that they could understand who they are and how they could achieve their divine destiny.[4] One might interpret this Gospel to have presented Jesus as the wandering sage except for its insistence that Jesus was categorically different from a sage. A wandering sage is radically different from a prophet who came from the Presence and who taught his audiences how they might reach the Presence.

The author of the Gospel of Thomas presented the image of Jesus as having the characteristics of the Christ. Moreover, the author presented that image of the Christ very early, even before the evangelists had fashioned their images that would eventually be taken as the conventional norms for so identifying Jesus as the Christ.

XIV The Christ of Faith

This search into the early data of the Christian community's belief revealed that, to associate Jesus with the Presence in striking ways, the community developed an explosion of devotions to him. In the process they formulated a mutation or variant form of their traditional monotheistic practice. The members of the early Christian community were Jews who emerged from a Jewish tradition that had formed them to be passionately committed to monotheism.

Despite this, devotion to Jesus as the Christ of God emerged very soon after the crucifixion; it was indeed not a late development. As far as historical inquiry permits one to say, it was an immediate characteristic in the belief and devotions of the circles of those who first identified themselves as followers of Jesus.[1] The evidence indicates that Bultmann had been rather hasty in proposing that belief in Jesus as the Christ was a development in the later church. The very early belief in Jesus as the Christ suggests that those who had known him must have fashioned their beliefs and devotions to him as the Christ because they had agreed that Jesus had accepted such a self-designation. It is difficult to imagine that those who knew Jesus and considered themselves committed to him would have allowed such belief and devotions to develop unless Jesus had somehow initiated that belief and those devotions.

Jesus Christ and Monotheism

The earliest believers (30 to 50 CE) characteristically sought to understand and express Jesus' divine significance in relation to the one God. In their religious thought—that is, in the ways they defined and portrayed Jesus in their teachings—they usually referred to him with reference to God: God's Son, the Christ of God, the Messiah of God, the Word of God, the Image of God, the Servant of God, redeemer, or eschatological prophet.[2] Their very early identity of Jesus as bonded with the one God probably developed from the identity of self that Jesus himself had promoted.

Christ as Fulfillment of the Hebrew Scriptures

The early believers began almost immediately to seek through the Hebrew Scriptures for passages that Jesus had fulfilled. Very soon they identified Psalm 22:16–18:

> For dogs are all around me;
>   a company of evildoers encircles me.
> My hands and feet have shriveled;
> I can count all my bones.
> They stare and gloat over me;
> they divide my clothes among themselves,
>   and for my clothing they cast lots.

Believers concluded that in his crucifixion Jesus had fulfilled this scripture's prediction of the promised Messiah. They similarly cited Psalm 118.

However, they found that the most suitable texts from the Hebrew Scriptures were the four songs of the Suffering Servant by Second Isaiah (Isa 42:1–4; 49:1–6; 50:4–9; 52:13—53:12). For example:

> See, my servant....
> Just as there were many who were astonished at him
>   —so marred was his appearance, beyond human semblance,
>   and his form beyond that of mortals....
>
> He had no form or majesty that we should look at him,
>   nothing in his appearance that we should desire him.
> He was despised and rejected by others;
>   a man of suffering and acquainted with infirmity;
> and as one from whom others hide their faces
>   he was despised and we held him of no account.

Those earliest followers of Jesus had recognized him as having not only fulfilled, but as having intended to fulfill, the expectations that Second Isaiah had fashioned in the songs of the Suffering Servant for the one who would be the Promised One.

The Gospels of Mark and Matthew: Jesus as the Christ

Fifty years after the crucifixion, the Evangelist Mark identified Jesus as "Jesus Christ, the Son of God" (Mark 1:1). Ten years later, the Evangelist Matthew also identified Jesus as "Jesus the Messiah, the son of David, the son of Abraham" (Matt 1:1).

Then in his fashioning of the Sermon on the Mount, Matthew envisioned Jesus as having had an indisputable authority to radically reinterpret the manner in which believers were to reform their obedience to the Presence. Matthew's words of Jesus included, "You have heard that it was said to those of ancient times, 'You shall not murder'; and 'whoever murders shall be liable to judgment.' But I say to you that if you are angry with a brother or sister, you will be liable to judgment" (Matt 5:21–22). In that sermon, Matthew had Jesus often repeat the formula "you have heard that it was said…but I say to you…." to manifest that he exercised the authority of the prophet, the Promised One.[3]

Later, Matthew envisioned John the Baptist's disciples as having come to Jesus when the Baptist was in prison and as having asked Jesus: "Are you he who is to come?" Jesus responded by citing the actions that the Presence was doing through Jesus: "The blind receive their sight, the lame walk, the lepers are cleansed, the deaf hear, the dead are raised, and the poor have good news brought to them" (Matt 11:3, 5). Those were the works that Second Isaiah (Isa 29:18–19; 35:5–6; 61:1) had predicted that the Messiah would do. Not only did Matthew identify Jesus as the Messiah, but also as the one fulfilling the expected roles of the Promised One.

However, despite identifying Jesus as the Messiah, Matthew presented Jesus as a Christ who is radically different from the expected Messiah. Jesus was not a political and military victor, but a victim of persecution. Jesus the Christ did not perform the expected messianic works of military force and political power.[4]

At the very end of Matthew's Gospel, the Evangelist had Jesus promise, "And remember, I am with you always, to the end of the age" (Matt 28:20). Matthew's vision of Jesus the Christ included his divine power to remain present to the community in a transcendent manner.[5]

Thus, from the third generation after the death of Jesus (Matthew's Gospel was written in about 85 CE), Jesus was for the community not only the Christ, but the one who acts for the Presence in that manner that the Presence, not conventional beliefs, had chosen for him.

Luke's Gospel: Jesus the Christ

Similarly, at the same time as Matthew, the Evangelist Luke identified Jesus as "Lord." For instance, Luke's Elizabeth greeted Mary who was with child, "And why has this happened to me, that the mother of my Lord comes to me?" (Luke 1:43).

Further, as Matthew did, Luke portrayed Jesus as having claimed to be the prophet.

> At that very hour some Pharisees came and said to him, "Get away from here, for Herod wants to kill you." He said to them, "Go and tell that fox for me, 'Listen, I am casting out demons and performing cures today and tomorrow, and the third day I finish my work. Yet today and tomorrow and the next day I must be on my way, because it is impossible for a prophet to be killed outside of Jerusalem.'" (Luke 13:31–33)

The prophet had spoken.[6]

That gospel form of revering Jesus as a prophet emerged when the community was still conscious of the kind of individual the historical Jesus had presented himself to be: not in the expected form of the Messiah (as the new David, or a political and military victor) but rather as the prophet who confronted his adversaries and permitted himself to become vulnerable to their persecution.

Second Generation of the Community

Gradually, a generation separated the members of the community from the event of the crucifixion. In that time the term *Lord* as applied to Jesus took on the connotation of Jesus' having been exalted by God, who raised him up into a glory that is eschatological—not yet fully realized—and heavenly—far greater in that realm than in the realm on earth.[7] That development of the interpretation of Jesus as the Christ confirms part of Bultmann's hypothesis, namely, that the Christ of faith emerged from a development of Christian theology. However, Jesus had been identified as the Christ of faith almost immediately after his death. Therefore, he must himself have laid the foundation for the designation of Christ.

Prior even to Paul's letters (50 to 60 CE), the Jerusalem community had customarily identified Jesus by various titles as united with the one God. The community within one generation of Jesus' execution as a civil criminal had taken the extraordinary step of confessing Jesus and the Father as a "binitry," or two-personed, God. Their bold choice to reformulate the traditionally sacred monotheistic identity of the Presence suggests that Jesus had presented his personal relationship with the Presence as a peer and that the earliest followers had remembered Jesus as having taught them that the Father and he are one.[8] To the extent that such an argument rests on solid data and develops along firm lines, there needs to be a new thesis regarding the Christ of faith: Jesus himself revealed himself to be, not only the Christ of the Presence, but even the peer of the Presence.

Christ in Paul's Letters

Scarcely more than a year after Jesus' execution, the "Jesus movement" had attracted the ire of Jewish religious zealots such as Saul of Tarsus. Furthermore, Saul also claimed that his later conversion to the Jesus movement had led to his capitulation to a very high view of Jesus: "God was pleased to…reveal his Son to me" (Gal 1:15–16).[9] One might suspect that the other apostles, in their desperate need for hope, had projected that hope into a resurrection of Jesus after the crucifixion; they might have so wanted their Master to be victorious that they

imagined him to have risen from the dead. However, one cannot interpret the conversion of Saul that way. Saul had no emotional investment
in Jesus; he had a commitment to destroy the Jesus movement. Yet
even such an enemy of the Jesus movement converted to believing in
the resurrection and to joining the Jesus movement because, as he
claimed, "God was pleased to…reveal his Son to me."

Such a conversion gives one ground to infer that the basis for
Christ's having been identified as the Christ was a consequence of the
Risen One's having manifested himself as the Christ both to the anti-
Christian Paul and to the other apostles within a very few days or years
of his death.

As a personal response to that manifestation of the crucified and
then Risen One as the Christ, Saul changed his name to that of the
"apostle Paul." Paul then identified the Risen One who had encountered him in an appearance as "Jesus Christ" (Gal 1:12). That, hence-
forth, became the name by which the crucified and risen Lord was
known by the entire early community.[10]

The Risen One had so profoundly transformed the belief of those
whom he encountered that they had fashioned that new manner of
referring to him.

Also within that first generation after Jesus' death but prior to Paul's
conversion, the community developed a pattern of devotion to Jesus.[11]
Paul's letters manifest traces of that devotion, such as mutual sharing of
goods as a response to the Lord's emphasis upon communal charity. The
community's evolution into being a group of those who practiced charity and love for one another influenced Paul's vision of the Jesus who had
founded that movement. Paul understood the Christ to have been and to
continue to be the prophet of communal charity. Thereafter, Paul's practice of appending *Christ* to the name *Jesus* manifested that early Christian
vision of the prophet of love and influenced the manner in which Paul
later developed that vision.

Furthermore, in 1 Corinthians, Paul maintained a totally negative
stance toward worship of anyone or anything other than the "one God,
the Father, from whom are all things and for whom we exist, and the
one Lord, Jesus Christ" (1 Cor 8:6). Paul's easy inclusion of devotion to
Christ within his emphatically monotheistic posture illustrates the
intriguing nature of early binitarian devotion to Christ. It was a devotion seemingly incompatible with a vigorous monotheistic faith and

practice. Yet Jesus did not become for the early believers an additional god. Rather, they reverenced him as in relationship to the one God. Jesus for them functioned (and still functions) as God's principal agent. He revealed God and acted redemptively on God's authority, acted as expressing God's will and serving God's purposes and glory.[12]

Paul's creative theology emerges in his novel designation of the Risen One as Jesus Christ: the Christ is understood to be the Christ of God, not an alternate deity.

Communal Experiences of Christ

One cannot but ask why Christ-devotion assumed the proportions that it did: a radically new binitarian devotional pattern that was unprecedented in Jewish monotheism. A second figure, Jesus Christ, was included with God in the devotional pattern of the Christian community.

A plausible basis for that was the powerful religious experiences in the early community of the Risen One's revelatory validity and force, experiences that must have been sufficiently transforming to demand such a reconfiguring of monotheism.

Again, one may find Paul's citing of that experience in 1 Corinthians. Scarcely twenty years after the crucifixion, Paul recited a sacred tradition as the creed regarding Jesus. The tradition confessed that Jesus had died redemptively for our sins, that he was raised on the third day in accordance with the scriptures, and that he appeared to a series of chosen figures (1 Cor 15:1–11). Those appearances must have been such powerful experiences that they contributed significantly to the community's binitarian convictions about Jesus. The community was convinced that Jesus Christ has an exalted and unique heavenly status; that he presides by God's appointment over the redemption; and that he now has divine-like glory.[13] All those Christ-characteristics were acknowledged to belong to the Risen One because of the experiences of him by chosen members of the very early community.

Moreover, Paul wrote that he had received (from the community) those beliefs regarding the Risen One. This means that the community had settled upon the binitarian devotion by the time that Paul wrote. Within twenty years of Jesus' death, believers identified the Risen One as uniquely bound together with the one God.

Paul himself formulated those convictions through pondering the community's meaning of the death of the one who had appeared to select members, including himself. Paul expressed that meaning as "Christ died for our sins" (1 Cor 15:3).[14] Before the community had formulated a normative doctrinal organization, its members had been formed by the earliest experiences of the Risen One to confess him to be the Christ of God.

The Glorification of Christ Crucified

Crucifixion was the most horrible of executions. No Roman citizen could be crucified. Eventually Rome decided that crucifixion was too degrading of an execution for anyone to receive. Yet Jesus of Nazareth had been crucified. Perhaps the horror of Jesus' death had led Paul to find an interpretation for why Jesus had suffered that ignominious fate. Paul drew from the Hebrew Scriptures, especially from the psalms and Second Isaiah, the interpretation of the crucifixion as the fulfillment of God's plan, revealed "according to the scriptures." Paul's formulation of that plan— Jesus was given over for our trespasses and raised for our justification (Rom 4:25)—came from the vision of Second Isaiah in the fourth song of the Suffering Servant (Isa 52:13—53:12).[15]

See, my servant shall prosper;
  he shall be exalted and lifted up,
  and shall be very high.
Just as there were many who were astonished at him
  —so marred was his appearance, beyond human semblance,
  and his form beyond that of mortals—
so he shall startle many nations;
  kings shall shut their mouths because of him;
for that which had not been told them they shall see,
  and that which they had not heard they shall contemplate.
Who has believed what we have heard?
  And to whom has the arm of the LORD been revealed?
For he grew up before him like a young plant,
  and like a root out of dry ground;
he had no form or majesty that we should look at him,

nothing in his appearance that we should desire him.
He was despised and rejected by others;
    a man of suffering and acquainted with infirmity;
and as one from whom others hide their faces
    he was despised, and we held him of no account.

Surely he has borne our infirmities
    and carried our diseases;
yet we accounted him stricken,
    struck down by God, and afflicted.
But he was wounded for our transgressions,
    crushed for our iniquities;
upon him was the punishment that made us whole,
    and by his bruises we are healed.
All we like sheep have gone astray;
    we have all turned to our own way,
and the LORD has laid on him
    the iniquity of us all.

He was oppressed, and he was afflicted,
    yet he did not open his mouth;
like a lamb that is led to the slaughter,
    and like a sheep that before its shearers is silent,
    so he did not open his mouth.
By a perversion of justice he was taken away.
    Who could have imagined his future?
For he was cut off from the land of the living,
    stricken for the transgression of my people.
They made his grave with the wicked
    and his tomb with the rich,
although he had done no violence,
    and there was no deceit in his mouth.

Yet it was the will of the LORD to crush him with pain.
When you make his life an offering for sin,
    he shall see his offspring, and shall prolong his days;
through him the will of the LORD shall prosper.
    Out of his anguish he shall see light;

he shall find satisfaction through his knowledge.
>   The righteous one, my servant, shall make many righteous;
>   and he shall bear their iniquities.
> Therefore I will allot him a portion with the great,
>   and he shall divide the spoil with the strong;
> because he poured out himself to death,
>   and was numbered with the transgressors;
> yet he bore the sin of many,
>   and made intercession for the transgressors.

John's gospel portrayal of the crucifixion of Jesus drew heavily upon that Servant Song by Second Isaiah. The nineteenth chapter of John's Gospel includes several passages that appear to have been drawn from it. John, influenced by Paul's use of the fourth Servant Song, used passages from it to demonstrate that Jesus had offered himself as the premier servant of the Presence in his having meekly accepted the degradation of the crucifixion. Thus, as the Servant Song foresaw, the Presence responded to Jesus' self-offering by raising up the servant Jesus or, in John's word, by glorifying Jesus.

The expression of faith in the Servant as Savior long predated the formation of the Christian community. The community chose to identify the Risen One as having fulfilled the promises of this Savior in Deutero-Isaiah's vision in the Hebrew Scriptures.

Moreover, Paul also referred to Jesus Christ as "the Son" (Rom 8:32). In view of the texts from Qumran, discovered in the Holy Land in 1947, it now seems that divine sonship was part of the royal-messianic rhetoric of pre-Christian Judaism. Divine sonship did not function to connote divinity; however, it certainly indicated a special status and relationship to God. Paul acknowledged Jesus to have that status and relationship.[16] At the earliest date of the community's formulation of its language for the Risen One, it adopted Paul's formulation of "the Son," drawn from the Hebrew Scriptures. This signifies that the earliest members of the community along with Paul understood the ministry, the execution, and the rising of the Christ (the Messiah) to have been redemptive for all humans.

The Gospel of John: Jesus the Christ

Toward the end of the first century, the Evangelist John presented a Gospel that was largely independent of the Synoptic tradition. Even so, John still identified Jesus as the Christ "of God." That "high Christology" of the Johannine community may date from after 70 CE, when the community became more Gentile than Jewish. Increasingly, the Gentile believers in the community began to identify Jesus as a god, as a second deity alongside the God of the Bible.[17] The Gospel indeed fashioned many passages that expressed the belief that Jesus was God.

For example, in the passage depicting Jesus' conversation with the woman of Samaria, Jesus responded to the woman, "If you knew the gift of God and who it is that is saying to you, 'Give me a drink,' you would have asked him, and he would have given you living water" (John 4:10). The Evangelist directed his vision of Jesus against those who viewed Jesus as only a human.[18]

While one can certainly seek to interpret the motivation behind the Evangelist's insistence that Jesus is divine, one cannot ignore the early first-century belief that Jesus Christ is far more than a human, is in fact the Christ of God.

New Testament Faith in Christ

The Synoptic Gospels portrayed Jesus as having come into conflict with his contemporaries because of some of his actions. Mark 2:1–12 presented a clash between Jesus and his fellow Jews because Jesus forgave sins. The same Evangelist focused upon the conflict between the observant Jews and Jesus because Jesus associated with "sinners" (Mark 2:13–17), defended those who did not fast (Mark 2:18–22), and reinterpreted the meaning of the Sabbath (Mark 2:23—3:6). Later in his Gospel, Mark portrayed Jesus as challenging the traditions about diet in the Law (Mark 7:1–23). The underlying issue in all of those confrontations is the Gospel's portrayal of Jesus as having the extraordinary authority that only the Christ would have. Indeed, some Jews refused to acknowledge that Jesus had such authority.[19] Yet those who confessed New Testament faith had only the one image of Jesus, namely, he is the Christ who possesses (present tense) the exalted authority that he receives from the Presence.

The Gospels, moreover, presented Jesus in an eschatological perspective: he was already the Christ, but not yet fully the Christ he would be. The evangelists foresaw a decisive future victory of the Christ in the Presence's purposes over all evil and over all that opposes the Presence's saving design. So too the Gospels presented the Kingdom of God as eschatological. Jesus' actions inaugurated the Kingdom, as evidenced by exorcisms, healings, and forgiveness of sinners. They portrayed Jesus as the special vehicle, the Promised One, through whom the purposes of the Kingdom of the Presence on earth are being realized.[20] The evangelists insisted that Jesus was not simply another human individual but the Promised One, because of whom human history turns now in a new direction.

Finally, the New Testament presented Jesus as having preexisted his conception and birth. That preexistence, however, was not a philosophical or mystical speculation on the part of the authors. Rather, they insisted in their belief that the Christ had always been with the Presence, who sent the Christ forth to earth as Jesus of Nazareth. Paul's Letter to the Philippians (Phil 2:6–7) was chronologically the first such confession of faith that Jesus is the eternal Christ. Then Paul's 1 Corinthians (1 Cor 8:6) linked the Christ with the first moment of creation. The Evangelist John's prologue (John 1:1–18) revealed that the community, forty years after Paul's letters, continued to maintain faith in Jesus as the eternal Christ.[21] Long before the church assumed a dogmatic role, the New Testament had portrayed Jesus of Nazareth as the very highly exalted Christ of faith.

Jewish Christians' Binitarian Worship of Jesus

While after 70 CE there were increasing numbers of Gentile Christians, the community had begun as exclusively Jewish, made up of believers who were defiantly monotheistic. Jews refused to worship any but the one God of Israel. They acknowledged no other deities or divine agents of other peoples as having validity. Nonetheless, they worshipped Jesus Christ as deserving of cultic devotion; that was a step that cannot be accounted for on the basis of the tendencies in the

Roman-era Jewish religion. Those monotheistic Jews insistently worshipped Jesus. Obviously they had reconfigured the monotheistic tradition so as to accommodate Jesus with God as the rightful recipient of worship.[22] The Spirit of Christ who moved within the community led the Jewish believers in the first century to develop a form of worship of Jesus that would have shocked those who espoused only the strict monotheism of the Jews.

Alexandria's Jesus as Divine

In the early second century, Christianity had developed roots in Alexandria of northern Africa. The writings of Christians in Alexandria, such as Valentinian (c. 100–175 CE), insisted that the historic Jesus is himself the divine Son and the paramount divine revelation to humanity.[23] One might again seek historical roots for such a high Christology in second-century Alexandria. Nonetheless, one cannot ignore that the believing community there had continued the Johannine community's firm belief that the Jesus of history is God.

The Early Tension in Identifying Jesus Christ

Alongside the vision of Jesus Christ as divine in the Johannine and the Alexandrian communities, there continued to be the vision of Jesus Christ as human. That belief has traditionally been associated with the Christian community in Antioch (of Syria).

That polarization in identifying Jesus developed perhaps because of something in Jesus' own historical actions and statements, something that generated or at least contributed to a polarization in his identity. The gospel narratives certainly make the royal-messianic charge against Jesus as the basis of his execution (Mark 15:10–26; Luke 23:1, 32–38; Matthew 27:11–14, 20–23, 37; John 18:33–37, 19:12).[24] On the other hand, the Gospels depict Jesus as being angry, fearful, frustrated, and physically tired: those are experiences that identify him as a human being. Indeed, the ground for a polarized identification of Jesus was written into the good news about Jesus.

Jesus of History as Christ of Faith

Rudolf Bultmann in the first half of the twentieth century argued convincingly that the Jesus of history was discrete from the Christ of faith, that the Christ of faith had been created by the early church. However, the investigations and inferences of the Jesus Seminar uncovered persuasive arguments that the Jesus of history had presented himself as the Christ of faith. The early church had carried over that presentation from the teachings of Jesus into the creedal confessions of the church.

Notes

Chapter One

1. Rudolf Bultmann, "New Testament and Mythology: The Problem of Demythologizing the New Testament Proclamation," in *New Testament and Mythology and Other Basic Writings*, ed. Schubert M. Ogden (London: SCM Press, 1985), 21.

2. Rudolf Bultmann, "The Significance of the Historical Jesus for the Theology of Paul," in *Faith and Understanding*, ed. Robert W. Funk, trans. Louise Pettibone Smith (London: SCM Press, Ltd., 1966), 238, 239, 260, 261.

3. James D. G. Dunn, "Can the Third Quest Hope to Succeed?" in *Authenticating the Activities of Jesus*, eds. Bruce Chilton and Craig A. Evans (Leiden: Brill, 1999), 46.

4. Ben F. Meyer, *The Aims of Jesus* (San Jose, CA: Pickwick Publishers, 2002), 81–82.

5. John P. Meier, *A Marginal Jew, vol. I: The Roots of the Problem and the Person* (New York: Doubleday, 1991), 174.

6. Meier, *A Marginal Jew, vol. I: The Roots of the Problem and the Person* , 168, 171–72, 174, 176, 177.

7. Meier, *A Marginal Jew, vol. I: The Roots of the Problem and the Person*, 176.

8. Meier, *A Marginal Jew, vol. I: The Roots of the Problem and the Person*, 177.

9. James D. G. Dunn, "Can the Third Quest Hope to Succeed?" in *Authenticating the Activities of Jesus*, eds. Bruce Chilton and Craig A. Evans (Leiden: Brill, 1999), 43.

10. Dunn, 45.

11. Dunn, 44–45.

12. Luke Timothy Johnson, *The Real Jesus: The Misguided Quest for the Historical Jesus and the Truth of the Traditional Gospels* (New York: HarperCollins Publishers, 1996), 107, 167.

13. James D. G. Dunn, "Can the Third Quest Hope to Succeed?" in *Authenticating the Activities of Jesus*, eds. Bruce Chilton and Craig A. Evans (Leiden: Brill, 1999), 33–34.

Chapter Two

1. James D. G. Dunn, "Can the Third Quest Hope to Succeed?" in *Authenticating the Activities of Jesus*, eds. Bruce Chilton and Craig A. Evans (Leiden: Brill, 1999), 45.

2. E. P. Sanders, *Jesus and Judaism* (Philadelphia: Fortress Press, 1985), 165.

3. E. P. Sanders, *Jesus and Judaism* (Philadelphia: Fortress Press, 1985), 165, 170, 172.

4. John P. Meier, *A Marginal Jew, vol. II: Mentor, Message, and Miracles* (New York: Doubleday, 1994), 237–39.

5. Meier, *A Marginal Jew, vol. II: Mentor, Message, and Miracles*, 240.

6. Meier, *A Marginal Jew, vol. II: Mentor, Message, and Miracles*, 241.

7. Meier, *A Marginal Jew, vol. II: Mentor, Message, and Miracles*, 289.

8. Meier, *A Marginal Jew, vol. II: Mentor, Message, and Miracles*, 330–34.

9. N. T. Wright, *The Challenge of Jesus: Rediscovering Who Jesus Was and Is* (Downers Grove, IL: Intervarsity Press, 1999), 48–50.

10. Sanders, 142–43.

11. Sanders, 231.

12. Meier, *A Marginal Jew, vol. II: Mentor, Message, and Miracles*, 307–8.

13. Ben F. Meyer, *The Aims of Jesus* (San Jose, CA: Pickwick Publishers, 2002), 132.

14. Sanders, 174–78.

15. Sanders, 227.

16. Sanders, 206–8.

17. Sanders, 210.

18. John P. Meier, *A Marginal Jew, vol. III: Companions and Competitors* (New York: Doubleday, 2001), 493–4.

19. Meier, *A Marginal Jew, vol. II: Mentor, Message, and Miracles*, 429.

20. Meier, *A Marginal Jew, vol. II: Mentor, Message, and Miracles*, 291.

21. Sanders, 152.

22. Meyer, *The Aims of Jesus* 151.

23. Sanders, 153.

24. Sanders, 157–58.

25. Sanders, 164.

26. Meier, *A Marginal Jew, vol. II: Mentor, Message, and Miracles*, 313–16.

27. Meier, *A Marginal Jew, vol. II: Mentor, Message, and Miracles*, 411–12.

28. Meyer, *The Aims of Jesus*, 140–41.

29. Meier, *A Marginal Jew, vol. II: Mentor, Message, and Miracles*, 439–41.

30. Meier, *A Marginal Jew, vol. II: Mentor, Message, and Miracles*, 294–96.

31. Meier, *A Marginal Jew, vol. II: Mentor, Message, and Miracles*, 300.

Chapter Three

1. E. P. Sanders, *Jesus and Judaism* (Philadelphia: Fortress Press, 1985), 16.

2. Sanders, 18, 22.

3. John P. Meier, *A Marginal Jew, vol. III: Companions and Competitors* (New York: Doubleday, 2001), 62–63.

4. Meier, *A Marginal Jew, vol. III: Companions and Competitors*, 64–66.

5. Ben F. Meyer, *The Aims of Jesus* (San Jose, CA: Pickwick Publishers, 2002), 130.

6. Meier, *A Marginal Jew, vol. III: Companions and Competitors*, 67–72.

7. Meyer, *The Aims of Jesus*, 169.

8. J. Ramsey Michaels, "The Itinerant Jesus and His Home Town," in *Authenticating the Activities of Jesus*, eds. Bruce Chilton and Craig A. Evans (Leiden: Brill, 1999), 186–87.

9. Robert W. Funk, Roy W. Hoover, and the Jesus Seminar, *The Five Gospels: The Search for the Authentic Words of Jesus* (New York: Macmillan Publishing Co., 1993), 30–31.

10. Meyer, *The Aims of Jesus*, 155–56.

11. Funk, Hoover, and the Jesus Seminar, 4.

12. Funk, Hoover, and the Jesus Seminar, 21.

13. Funk, Hoover, and the Jesus Seminar, 29–30.

14. Funk, Hoover, and the Jesus Seminar, 22–25.

15. Funk, Hoover, and the Jesus Seminar, 19–21.

16. Michaels, 177.

17. Funk, Hoover, and the Jesus Seminar, 24–25.

18. Funk, Hoover, and the Jesus Seminar, 24–25.

19. Sanders, 71–73.

20. James Marcus, "The Beelzebul Controversy and the Eschatologies of Jesus," in *Authenticating the Activities of Jesus*, eds. Bruce Chilton and Craig A. Evans (Leiden: Brill, 1999), 273.

21. Sanders, 109.

22. Sanders, 115–19.

Chapter Four

1. Ben F. Meyer, *The Aims of Jesus* (San Jose, CA: Pickwick Publishers, 2002), 75.

2. E. P. Wright, *Jesus and the Victory of God* (Minneapolis: Fortress Press, 1996), 154–55.

3. Meyer, *The Aims of Jesus*, 164–65.

4. E. P. Sanders, *Jesus and Judaism* (Philadelphia: Fortress Press, 1985), 11.

5. Craig Evans, "Authenticating the Activities of Jesus," in Bruce Chilton and Craig A. Evans, eds., *Authenticating the Activities of Jesus* (Leiden: Brill, 1999), 11.

6. Meyer, *The Aims of Jesus*, 122.

7. N. T. Wright, *The Challenge of Jesus: Rediscovering Who Jesus Was and Is* (Downers Grove, IL: Intervarsity Press, 1999), 38–39.

8. Marcus Ellis, "Public Action," in *Authenticating the Activities of Jesus*, eds. Bruce Chilton and Craig A. Evans (Leiden: Brill, 1999), 56–57.

9. N. T. Wright, 38.

10. Bruce Chilton, "An Exorcism of History," in Bruce Chilton and Craig A. Evans, eds., *Authenticating the Activities of Jesus* (Leiden: Brill, 1999), 223–25.

11. Sanders, 75.

12. Craig Evans, "Jesus and Zechariah's Messianic Hope," in Bruce Chilton and Craig A. Evans, eds., *Authenticating the Activities of Jesus* (Leiden: Brill, 1999), 382–83.

13. Martin Hengel, "Jesus, the Messiah of Israel," in Bruce Chilton and Craig A. Evans, eds., *Authenticating the Activities of Jesus* (Leiden: Brill, 1999), 323–49.

14. Meyer, *The Aims of Jesus*, 123.

15. Martin Hengel, "Jesus, the Messiah of Israel," in Bruce Chilton and Craig A. Evans, eds., *Authenticating the Activities of Jesus* (Leiden: Brill, 1999), 341–42.

16. Bruce Malina, "Assessing the Historicity of Jesus' Walking on Water," in Bruce Chilton and Craig A. Evans, eds., *Authenticating the Activities of Jesus* (Leiden: Brill, 1999), 355–57.

17. Craig A. Evans, "Authenticating the Activities of Jesus," in Bruce Chilton and Craig A. Evans, eds., *Authenticating the Activities of Jesus* (Leiden: Brill, 1999), 28–29.

18. J. Ramsey Michaels, "The Itinerant Jesus and His Home Town," in Bruce Chilton and Craig A. Evans, eds., *Authenticating the Activities of Jesus* (Leiden: Brill, 1999), 189.

19. N. T. Wright, 42–45.

20. Robert W. Funk, Roy W. Hoover, and the Jesus Seminar, *The Five Gospels: The Search for the Authentic Words of Jesus* (New York: Macmillan Publishing Co., 1993), 32.

21. Craig A. Evans, "Authenticating the Activities of Jesus," in Bruce Chilton and Craig A. Evans, eds., *Authenticating the Activities of Jesus* (Leiden: Brill, 1999), 23–26.

22. Joel Marcus, "The Beezebul Controversy and the Eschatologies of Jesus," in Bruce Chilton and Craig A. Evans, eds., *Authenticating the Activities of Jesus* (Leiden: Brill, 1999), 247, 253, 263.

23. Meyer, *The Aims of Jesus*, 159–62.

24. Bruce Chilton and Craig A. Evans, eds., *Authenticating the Activities of Jesus* (Leiden: Brill, 1999), 279, 298.

25. Craig A. Evans, "Authenticating the Activities of Jesus," in Bruce Chilton and Craig A. Evans, eds., *Authenticating the Activities of Jesus* (Leiden: Brill, 1999), 16–17.

26. Meyer, *The Aims of Jesus*, and N. T. Wright, *The Challenge of Jesus: Rediscovering Who Jesus Was and Is* (Downers Grove, IL: Intervarsity Press, 1999).

27. Sanders, 91–93.

28. Sanders, 79.

29. Sanders, 61–71.

30. Dale C. Allison, Jr., "Behind the Temptations of Jesus," in Bruce Chilton and Craig A. Evans, eds., *Authenticating the Activities of Jesus* (Leiden: Brill, 1999), 208–13.

31. Richard Bauckham, "Did Jesus Wash His Disciples' Feet?" in Bruce Chilton and Craig A. Evans, eds., *Authenticating the Activities of Jesus* (Leiden: Brill, 1999), 412–29.

Chapter Five

1. John P. Meier, *A Marginal Jew, vol. II: Mentor, Message, and Miracles* (New York: Doubleday, 1994), 407.

2. Herbert Jenning Rose and Anthony J. S. Spawforth, "Apollonius of Tyana," in *The Oxford Companion to Classical Civilization*, eds. Simon Hornblower and Anthony Spawforth (Oxford: Oxford University Press, 1998), 133.

3. Meier, *A Marginal Jew, vol. II: Mentor, Message, and Miracles*, 619.

4. Meier, *A Marginal Jew, vol. II: Mentor, Message, and Miracles*, 620.

5. John P. Meier, *A Marginal Jew, vol. I: The Roots of the Problem and the Person* (New York: Doubleday, 1991), 56–59.

6. Meier, *A Marginal Jew, vol. II: Mentor, Message, and Miracles*, 774.

7. Meier, *A Marginal Jew, vol. II: Mentor, Message, and Miracles*, 544.

8. Meier, *A Marginal Jew, vol. II: Mentor, Message, and Miracles*, 161, 630.

9. Meier, *A Marginal Jew, vol. II: Mentor, Message, and Miracles*, 648–52.

10. Meier, *A Marginal Jew, vol. II: Mentor, Message, and Miracles*, 934, 965, 966.

11. Meier, *A Marginal Jew, vol. II: Mentor, Message, and Miracles*, 78–79.

Chapter Six

1. E. P. Sanders, *Jesus and Judaism* (Philadelphia: Fortress Press, 1985), 252–54.

2. John P. Meier, *A Marginal Jew, vol. III: Companions and Competitors* (New York: Doubleday, 2001), 525–30.

3. Sanders, 257.

4. Sanders, 255–60.

5. Sanders, 249–50.

Chapter Seven

1. John P. Meier, *A Marginal Jew, vol. III: Companions and Competitors* (New York: Doubleday, 2001)), 496–97.

2. Ben F. Meyer, *The Aims of Jesus* (San Jose, CA: Pickwick Publishers, 2002), 176–80.

3. Meyer, *The Aims of Jesus*, 209.

4. N. T. Wright, *The Challenge of Jesus: Rediscovering Who Jesus Was and Is* (Downers Grove, IL: Intervarsity Press, 1999), 86.

5. Wright, 83.

6. Wright, 112–13.

7. Meier, *A Marginal Jew, vol. III: Companions and Competitors*, 247.

8. Meyer, *The Aims of Jesus*, 135–36.

9. Meyer, *The Aims of Jesus*, 166–67.

10. Wright, 111–12.

11. Wright, 115.

12. Wright, 110–11.

13. Wright, 78–79.

14. Wright, 109.

Chapter Eight

1. Teilhard de Chardin, Pierre, *The Phenomenon of Man* (New York: Harper & Row, 1965).

2. N. T. Wright, *The Challenge of Jesus: Rediscovering Who Jesus Was and Is* (Downers Grove, IL: Intervarsity Press, 1999), 55.

3. John P. Meier, *A Marginal Jew, vol. III: Companions and Competitors* (New York: Doubleday, 2001), 152–54.

4. Wright, 65.

5. Wright, 68–69.

6. Meier, *A Marginal Jew, vol. III: Companions and Competitors*, 496.

7. Wright, 84.

8. Ben F. Meyer, *The Aims of Jesus* (San Jose, CA: Pickwick Publishers, 2002), 63–64.

9. E. P. Sanders, *Jesus and Judaism* (Philadelphia: Fortress Press, 1985), 325–27.

10. Wright, 58–65.

Chapter Nine

1. Larry W. Hurtado, *Lord Jesus Christ: Devotion to Jesus in Earliest Christianity* (Grand Rapids, MI: Eerdmans Publishing Co., 2003), 563.
2. Hurtado, 605.

Chapter Ten

1. E. P. Sanders, *Jesus and Judaism* (Philadelphia: Fortress Press, 1985), 218–21.

Chapter Eleven

1. John P. Meier, *A Marginal Jew, vol. III: Companions and Competitors* (New York: Doubleday, 2001), 142–43.
2. E. P. Sanders, *Jesus and Judaism* (Philadelphia: Fortress Press, 1985), 273.
3. Sanders, 275.
4. Sanders, 288–89.
5. Sanders, 271, 277.
6. Sanders, 270.
7. Sanders, 270–71.
8. Josephus, *Against Apion*, Steve Mason, ed. (Leiden: Brill, 2006), 11, 187.
9. Sanders, 316.
10. Sanders, 321–22.
11. McCana in *Authenticating the Activities of Jesus*, eds. Bruce Chilton and Craig A.Evans (Leiden: Brill, 1999), 436–40.

Chapter Twelve

1. Ben F. Meyer, *The Aims of Jesus* (San Jose, CA: Pickwick Publishers, 2002), 69, 73.
2. Meyer, *The Aims of Jesus*, 61–62.
3. N. T. Wright, *The Challenge of Jesus: Rediscovering Who Jesus Was and Is* (Downers Grove, IL: Intervarsity Press, 1999), 133–39.
4. Wright, 146.
5. Wright, 145.
6. Meyer, *The Aims of Jesus*, 65.

Chapter Thirteen

1. Robert W. Funk, Roy W. Hoover, and the Jesus Seminar, *The Five Gospels: The Search for the Authentic Words of Jesus* (New York: Macmillan Publishing Co., 1993), 18.

2. Larry W. Hurtado, *Lord Jesus Christ: Devotion to Jesus in Earliest Christianity* (Grand Rapids, MI: Eerdmans Publishing Co., 2003), 473.

3. Hurtado, 485.

4. Hurtado, 482.

Chapter Fourteen

1. Larry W. Hurtado, *Lord Jesus Christ: Devotion to Jesus in Earliest Christianity* (Grand Rapids, MI: Eerdmans Publishing Co., 2003), 2.

2. Hurtado, 3, 215.

3. Hurtado, 334.

4. John P. Meier, *A Marginal Jew, vol. II: Mentor, Message, and Miracles* (New York: Doubleday, 1994), 134–35.

5. Hurtado, 332.

6. Hurtado, 194.

7. Hurtado, 181.

8. Hurtado, 215.

9. Hurtado, 59.

10. Robert W. Funk, Roy W. Hoover, and the Jesus Seminar, *The Five Gospels: The Search for the Authentic Words of Jesus* (New York: Macmillan Publishing Co., 1993), 7.

11. Hurtado, 24.

12. Hurtado, 53.

13. Hurtado, 64–72.

14. Hurtado, 97.

15. Hurtado, 128.

16. Hurtado, 103.

17. Hurtado, 43.

18. Hurtado, 421.

19. Hurtado, 403.

20. Hurtado, 268–69.

21. Hurtado, 364–68.

22. Hurtado, 29–33.

23. Hurtado, 526.

24. Hurtado, 55–56.

Selected Bibliography

Bultmann, Rudolf. "New Testament and Mythology: The Problem of Demythologizing the New Testament Proclamation." In *New Testament and Mythology and Other Basic Writings*. Selected, edited, and translated by Schubert M. Ogden, London: SCM Press, 1985.

—————. "The Significance of the Historical Jesus for the Theology of Paul." In *Faith and Understanding*. Edited by Robert W. Funk. Translated by Louise Pettibone Smith. London: SCM Press, Ltd., 1966.

Chilton, Bruce, and Craig A. Evans, eds. *Authenticating the Activities of Jesus*. Leiden: Brill, 1999.

Funk, Robert W., Roy W. Hoover, and the Jesus Seminar. *The Five Gospels: The Search for the Authentic Words of Jesus*. New York: Macmillan Publishing Co., 1993.

Hurtado, Larry W. *Lord Jesus Christ: Devotion to Jesus in Earliest Christianity*. Grand Rapids, MI: Eerdmans Publishing Co., 2003.

Johnson, Luke Timothy. *The Real Jesus: The Misguided Quest for the Historical Jesus and the Truth of the Traditional Gospels*. New York: HarperCollins Publishers, 1996.

Meier, John P. *A Marginal Jew: Rethinking the Historical Jesus*. Vol. I, *The Roots of the Problem and the Person*. New York: Doubleday, 1991.

—————. *A Marginal Jew: Rethinking the Historical Jesus*. Vol. II, *Mentor, Message, and Miracles*. New York: Doubleday, 1994.

—————. *A Marginal Jew: Rethinking the Historical Jesus*. Vol. III, *Companions and Competitors*. New York: Doubleday, 2001.

Meyer, Ben F. *The Aims of Jesus*. San Jose, CA: Pickwick Publishers, 2002.

Sanders, E. P. *Jesus and Judaism*. Philadelphia: Fortress Press, 1985.

Wright, E. P. *Jesus and the Victory of God*. Minneapolis: Fortress Press, 1996.

Wright, N. T. *The Challenge of Jesus: Rediscovering Who Jesus Was and Is*. Downers Grove, IL: Intervarsity Press, 1999.

Index